Maximizing Profits Immediately

How to Dramatically Improve Your Company's Bottom Line

by

MATTHEW P. FIGGIE AND RICHARD A. SOLON
WITH ADAM C. SNYDER

Copyright © 2015 Matthew P. Figgie
MaxProfits Publishing
All rights reserved.
ISBN: 1484073916
ISBN-13: 9781484073919
Library of Congress Control Number: 2013907333
CreateSpace Independent Publishing Platform
North Charleston, South Carolina

Maximizing Profits Immediately: How to Dramatically Improve Your Company's Bottom Line by Matthew P. Figgie and Richard A. Solon, with Adam C. Snyder

www.maximizingprofitsimmediately.com

TABLE OF CONTENTS

LIST OF EXHIBITS

AUTHORS' NOTE

This primer was inspired by the life's work of Harry E. Figgie Jr., who passed away in July of 2009. In part, it is an update of his popular *Cutting Costs: An Executive's Guide to Increased Profits*, first published under a different title in 1983. But more than that, it is a testament to Harry's lifelong belief that with a focus on the proper priorities and on certain fundamental profit improvement strategies, U.S. manufacturing companies can compete successfully in the global environment.

This book, like its predecessor, is by no means intended as a comprehensive guide to the latest manufacturing strategies and techniques. It does, however, provide the fundamental underpinnings of any successful profit improvement program.

The strategies outlined in the following pages spell out a common-sense approach to maximizing profits that is equally applicable to businesses of all sizes and in all types of industries, from the Pennsylvania steel mill, to the web-based shopping mall. They are a testament to the pioneering efforts of Harry Figgie, but also to the culture of innovation and productivity that has always been a hallmark of American business.

For further information, please go to maximizingprofitsimmediately.com.

Matthew P. Figgie
Richard A. Solon
Adam C. Snyder

December 2014

FOREWORD

60 Years With the Guru of Profitable Improvement
by Mrs. Nancy F. Figgie

Harry always had a plan. We met in 1948 on a blind date when I was a junior at Northwestern University. He had already been in General Patton's 86th Infantry Division, had graduated Case Institute of Technology in Cleveland, and had just completed his first year at the Harvard Business School. When he proposed, he laid out what he wanted to do with his life -- to build a major American company from scratch. Neither one of us had any money in the bank. I told him I thought he was nuts, but let's go.

Harry was a man in a hurry. He took seriously his Dad's advice to learn how to make something and how to sell it, so his employment during the early years of our marriage included entry level sales and manufacturing assignments in the Midwest. At the same time, he attended two night schools simultaneously, one to get a Masters in Industrial Engineering from Case Institute of Technology, and another for a law degree from Cleveland-Marshall College of Law. He wanted to understand both the multiplying number of new laws and regulations that were coming into play, *and* the rapid advancements being made in manufacturing.

To pay for his education, Harry taught night courses in industrial procurement and marketing and I worked in advertising. I can still remember typing his school papers and masters thesis and taking notes for him at his Monday and Wednesday night law classes.

In 1953 Harry began a nine-year stint at the consulting firm, Booz Allen Hamilton, where he experienced virtually every kind of challenge a manufacturing company had to offer. Then in 1963 he cobbled together the financing to purchase an ailing sprinkler company. He spent the next 30 years turning it into a billion dollar corporation that touched the lives of most Americans, with products like Rawlings baseball equipment, American LaFrance fire trucks, and everything from bottling equipment to missile guidance systems.

Harry ran Figgie International the way he ran his private life, with a steadfast belief in keeping it simple, continuous improvement, and getting the job done with intensity and focus. At one point *Fortune* magazine named him America's second toughest boss. He would half-jokingly complain that he had come in second place, that he had to practice what he preached and try harder.

Continuous improvement was a constant theme at home and at work. Continue to educate yourself, continue to get better, we told our children and anyone else who would listen. Harry' employees, his business partners, and our friends and family knew if we said we were going to do something, we'd set out to do it. They may have had their doubts that we would be successful, but they never had to question our intentions.

Harry was a clear byproduct of his parents. His father had success in the automotive parts business as a rare combination of engineer and sales executive. His mother was a school teacher, and both parents stressed to him and his sister the importance of continuous learning. Harry did too, as a way to advance Figgie International, and the individual people who worked there. Even in the very early days of the public company, employees were encouraged to attend evening business classes – on their own time. You had to have passion, desire, and a willingness to meet us more than half way. *There ain't no such thing as a free lunch* (TANSTAAFL) became a corporate mantra, formalized into a nationwide economic education program that included "Ump's FWAT," a color annual report for children, and three-day TANSTAAFL economic education workshops for teachers. In 1975 Finance Magazine honored Harry with its Corporate Leadership Award for his involvement in education as a means to combat economic illiteracy, and in 1980 the company's economic education program was given the Freedoms Foundation Award.

We didn't have much of a social life during these years, but that was our choice. Dinners at home with our kids, talking about their school day and about the business were enough for us. In the first few years of building the company I sometimes felt like a single parent, but after that we managed to have plenty of family time. We used sports to bind our family together. One time I donned full catcher's gear and told our eldest son to let one loose. I fell backwards like a bowling pin, but jumped right back up. I think that represented our lives together. We didn't sit back and let people do things for us. We got right in there and got to work.

I was also *Harry's* backstop during these years. He used me as a sounding board because he knew he could count on me to tell him the truth – good, bad, or indifferent – and that I would come at a problem from a different perspective. That was a great comfort to someone whose days were filled with making dozens of decisions and negotiating at least that many personalities. He was never afraid to tell me that something had gone wrong that day. "Well, what are you going to do about it?" I'd ask him.

Harry knew he had support at home, and that he could always count on his family. My mother-in-law and I were the best of friends, and that meant a lot to Harry, who had lost his father when he was 16.

Harry was so smart, he could be two miles down the road while other people were still in the garage. That's when I occasionally put on the breaks so other people could catch up, urging him to pause and take stock. Sometimes in a fervor to get something done he had a tendency to want to smash through and just do it. That's when I'd suggest there might be a different way. It might just mean taking an extra five minutes to recognize a different point of view or another aspect of an issue.

I think Harry's proudest accomplishment was that at one time the public company employed more than 16,000 people. I pointed out to him that meant he was impacting the lives of probably 50,000 men, women, and children. Spouses were encouraged to get to know the company too, which made a big difference to morale. People knew they could put their hand in the air and get help – a hand up, not a hand out. At our family company, Clark Reliance, that tradition continues. We make a life coach available to anyone in need of medical or financial help or advocacy. Then it's up to them to take on the responsibility for themselves.

Harry and I based our lives on old-fashioned American values, just like the principles laid out in this book. I'm told that after some rocky years, U.S. manufacturing is now more than holding its own against intense worldwide competition. Harry wouldn't be surprised, and he'd be delighted to be lending a helping hand with this update of his life's work.

December 2014

Mrs. Nancy F. Figgie, a graduate of Northwestern University where she was president of her sorority and of Mortar Board, the women's national honor society, was married to Harry Figgie for more than 60 years, until his death in 2009.

PREFACE

In today's environment the need for companies to become more efficient in everything they do has never been greater. Profits are being squeezed not only by a difficult economy, but also by international competition. In this "flat" environment, the ability of countries like China and other emerging economies to manufacture products at very little expense, sometimes subsidized by their government, can be intimidating to U.S. manufacturers trying to compete. But they *can* compete. To do it, they need to eliminate waste, improve efficiencies, and demonstrate to their customers the value proposition of their products.

There is certainly no lack of comprehensive programs aimed at helping managers improve their operations. In fact, the number of available resources can be overwhelming. Books, magazines, and the worldwide web are filled with the likes of Six Sigma, network optimization, continuous flow processing, fishbone, Kaizen, and Kanban – and these are just a few of the latest terms managers responsible for corporate profits are expected to understand and implement. Many of these techniques have been branded by top consulting firms and are used by multinational corporations, sometimes at a cost of many millions of dollars. Other companies expend equally significant resources putting the latest management theories into their own comprehensive profit improvement programs.

There is great value in virtually all these strategies. Six Sigma and lean manufacturing have made world-class companies out of global giants GE and Motorola, among many others. But many companies – particularly those doing under $100 million in sales – may not have the financial wherewithal or inclination to implement these increasingly sophisticated techniques. There is also the intimidation factor. Names like Fishbone, Direct Material Optimization, and Discounted

Cash Flow sound like you need a PhD, or at least a high priced consultant, to understand.

Nothing could be further from the truth. *Maximizing Profits Immediately: How to Dramatically Improve Your Company's Bottom Line* pulls away the curtain to reveal that the building blocks of the latest profit improvement strategies can be found in the tried and true techniques that people like Harry E. Figgie Jr., and now this book's other two authors, have implemented so successfully for more than half a century. In fact, many of the most modern profit improvement terms correspond to the techniques that Harry E. Figgie Jr. honed as a Booz Allen consultant in the 1950s. *Kanban* or *pull production*, for example, are really just steps toward establishing accurate sales forecasting. *Just in Time* could be described as a way to utilize ABC Inventory Control.

We believe that without understanding the principles laid out in this book, these other programs have the wrong starting point, and their success will be problematic. That's because at their core, business improvement philosophies like Six Sigma and lean manufacturing need certain fundamental profit improvement tasks, like ratio analysis, ABC stratification, and value analysis, in order to be successful. A Six Sigma program, for example, will only be effective by first conducting a comprehensive ratio analysis in order to determine during which years the organization performed best in a variety of spending categories. Only then can Six Sigma goals be made and met. Likewise, lean manufacturing will not be particularly meaningful unless all those on the front lines charged with its implementation understand a few foundational principles that come into play well before any manufacturing actually begins.

In the worst instances, modern management concepts only serve to obfuscate their true genius: their simplicity and ease of implementation. *Maximizing Profits Immediately* will explain how Six Sigma and the like relate to our more fundamental profit improvement techniques. In the process, using simple, straightforward techniques anyone can learn in a few weeks, it will teach managers how to quickly put in place operational strategies that will continually work to maximize profits week after week, year after year.

Each chapter of *Maximizing Profits Immediately* is self-contained so that the book does not have to be read in one sitting and can be used as a reference to address a specific problem. Our goal is to provide hands-on, relevant skills to anyone working in business interested in maximizing the efficiency of their organizations, without the complexity or expense of most modern profit improvement campaigns.

The strategies and techniques described in the following pages can be implemented by a top executive of a small or midsize company without consultants, with the help only of the company's chief financial person. Regardless of a company's size, by following the methods described in this text, companies should be able to realize an across-the-board savings of at least 5 percent after the first 30 days, and at least 10 percent within the first year. And as will be demonstrated in the first chapter, a 5 percent reduction in costs can increase profits by 200 percent, if the savings can be preserved.

In the context of maximizing profits, we have set out to accomplish four goals:

1. To show that in today's economy, understanding and implementing a few foundational profit improvement techniques can mean the difference between red ink and black.

2. To lay out these techniques in a way every executive, at any size business, can understand.

3. To demonstrate that these techniques are the building blocks of modern management theories such as Six Sigma, Total Quality Improvement, and Lean Manufacturing, to name just a few.

4. To demonstrate that U.S. companies can definitely compete in our global economy.

This is not a book that will explain Six Sigma, TQM (total quality management), and the like in great detail. Instead, it will lay out certain principles and techniques that form the foundation of these modern management theories and that we believe must be understood before any of them can be implemented successfully.

Often we will be talking directly to top executives because in order to maximize profits we believe our strategies must be understood, supported, and championed by a company's top operations officer. Ultimately, however, *Maximizing Profits Immediately* is aimed at all company personnel responsible for profit improvement efforts – and that means each and every employee.

The common sense strategies spelled out in the following pages represent six decades of hands-on experience, trial and error, and profitable balance sheets. We sincerely hope, and passionately believe, that they can also help your organization to maximize its profits ... IMMEDIATELY.

INTRODUCTION

Nothing New Under the Sun

Definition of management:
The art of getting things done through people."[1]
Mary Parker Follett (1868–1933)

The best management is a true science, resting upon clearly defined laws, rules, and principles as a foundation. ... the fundamental principles of scientific management are applicable to all kinds of human activities, from our simplest individual acts, to the work of our great corporations. ... whenever these principles are correctly applied, results must follow which are truly astounding.[2]

Frederick Winslow Taylor (1856-1915)

Ecclesiastes tells us that there is nothing new under the sun.[3] For our purposes, humorist Ambrose Bierce at the turn of the last century probably said it best. "There is nothing new under the sun," he wrote, "but there are lots of old things we don't know."[4]

That we don't know them, however, is our own fault. Sound management theory and techniques have been around for at least

---

1. Vocational Business: Training, Developing and Motivating People by Richard Barrett, Business & Economics, 2003, p. 51

2. Frederick Winslow Taylor, *The Principles of Scientific Management* (New York: Harper Bros., 1911

3. Ecclesiastes 1:9 00 "The thing that hath been, it is that which shall be; and that which is done is that which shall be done: and there is no new thing under the sun."

4. *The Devil's Dictionary*, Ambrose Bierce, 1911

six thousand years, when the Egyptians were able to build the pyramids by creating not only a remarkable engineering design, but also a structure for their planning and managerial authority. Two thousand years later the Code of Hammurabi set out principles of control and responsibility, and in about 400 BC the Greeks introduced the scientific method on which all modern management theory is based.

In more recent times, Adam Smith's *The Wealth of Nations* (1776) discussed how organizations could be made significantly more efficient through the division of labor. As an example, Smith described how changes in processes could boost productivity in the production of pins. By analyzing the manufacturing steps involved, adding ten specialists, and increasing efficiencies, he showed how production could be increased from 200 pins per day, to 48,000. Not long afterwards, innovators like Eli Whitney (1765-1825) and James Watt (1736-1819) were writing about the importance of quality control procedures.

It wasn't until the 20th Century that the world witnessed the first true management craze – Taylorism, named after Frederick Taylor, author of the seminal work, *The Principles of Scientific Management*. Inspired by the rise of the Industrial Age, Taylor believed that by studying work methods and directing people more precisely, maximum prosperity could be obtained for both employer and employee. Taylor developed "scientific management theory" in which he espoused the careful specification, measurement, and standardization of all organizational assignments. Max Weber went a bit further by suggesting that organizations develop comprehensive and detailed standard operating procedures for all routine tasks.

In 1912 Yoichi Ueno introduced Taylorism to Japan and became the first management consultant of the "Japanese management style." But it was W. Edwards Deming, a former statistician for the U.S. Census Bureau, in his first lecture to the Union of Japanese Scientists and Engineers, who introduced the concept of "quality management" to that country. Profit, he preached, came from repeat customers, so every person in a company should be focused on making the highest quality product possible. The Japanese ran with the concept, contributing mightily to its post World War II economic boom.

It took about thirty years for U.S. businesses to catch on to Deming's quality management concepts, but then they did so with a vengence, embracing techniques like TQM (Total Quality Management), KAIZEN, Continuous Improvement, and Six Sigma, to name just a few. All of them were built on the backs of men like Adam Smith, Frederick Winslow Taylor, W. Edwards Deming, and Peter Drucker, and in the future there will likely be other ideas which will improve on today's latest methods. At this writing, lean manufacturing seems to be most in vogue. According to the *Industry Week's Manufacturing Performance Institute Census of Manufacturers,*[5] nearly 70 percent of all plants in the United States have adopted lean manufacturing as a way to improve their manufacturing processes. That's twice as popular as the second most popular improvement method, TQM.

But what are these new theories of management? Boiling them down to their essence tends to uncover their mystery. TQM, for example, is a management philosophy for continuously improving quality based on the idea that the quality of a company's products and processes is the responsibility of everyone involved in their creation. Lean manufacturing is a production practice developed by Toyota. It considers the expenditure of resources for any goal other than the creation of value to the end customer to be wasteful. It has evolved into a comprehensive term referring to any methodology aimed at maximizing value and eliminating waste.

In the following pages we will be describing the strategies and hands-on techniques necessary to understand these latest management programs. We believe all of them have as their building blocks the fundamental profit improvement techniques first developed into a comprehensive strategy by Harry E. Figgie, Jr. more than

---

5. http://www.industryweek.com/section.aspx?sectionid=10

half a century ago. Lean manufacturing, for example, needs ratio analysis. Kanban and Just In Time need ABC stratification. Direct Material Optimization needs a simple method of product redesign. And Six Sigma needs every one of these methods. *Maximizing Profits Immediately* will show managers of small and midsize manufacturing companies how to implement common sense and proven techniques to set realistic goals and achieve outstanding, measurable results without having to hire a legion of expensive consultants. In many cases we will also explain how our straightforward principles relate to the latest theories and jargon.

Another goal of this book is to debunk the myth that U.S. manufacturing is dead, that we can no longer compete in a global environment. We are here to tell you that reports of the demise of U.S. manufacturing are way premature.

There is no denying, of course, that manufacturing does not dominate the U.S. economy as it once did. During the past sixty years the percentage of U.S. employment in manufacturing has declined from about 50 percent, to about 9 percent. Measured by GDP, its share of the economy has fallen from more than 25 percent in the 1950's to about half that today.[6] The decline represents a profound shift; manufacturing will never again dominate the U.S. economy as it once did. But that's an old story. It's time to write a new script.

In large part, the notion that we continue to witness the collapse of U.S. manufacturing is a hangover from the first three years of this century, when the number of workers employed in manufacturing fell from about 17.3 million to about 13.5 million. Since 2003, however, the decline has leveled off to more modest, historic averages, and appears now to have been reversed. According to the Labor Department, U.S. manufacturing companies are now consistently adding jobs, and still account for about $50 billion in exports every month. By itself, the manufacturing sector would be the eighth largest economy in the world. More goods are made

---

6. These numbers are underreported, since they do not take into account that many large U.S. manufacturers have outsourced many of their accounting and human resource functions.

in the United States today than at any time in history, and U.S. output, revenue, profit, and return on investment are at all-time highs.

Today manufacturing directly employs nearly 12 million Americans (or 9 percent of the workforce) and supports another 6.6 million jobs in other sectors, such as accounting, wholesaling, transportation, finance, insurance, and real estate. In total, that's about one in every six private sector job. In fact, every dollar in a manufactured product's final sale supports $1.37 in other areas of the economy, the highest multiplier of any other sector. No wonder state and local communities prefer manufacturing plants over any other kind of investment.

U.S. manufacturing is on the upswing. Recent headlines report that giant U.S. companies like GE and Apple are beginning to bring some of their manufacturing capacity back to the United States. Less publicized is that thousands of small and midsize manufacturing companies are consistently profitable and aggressively compete with their international competition. How do they do it? By being better, leaner, faster, and yes, sometimes even less expensive than their foreign competition. Much of the credit goes to the consistent ability of U.S. manufacturers to raise productivity.

The old story was that higher labor costs made it almost impossible for U.S. manufacturers to compete. But direct labor represents only 5–15 percent of total costs in most manufacturing companies. While higher costs remain, particularly in employee benefits, tort claims, and government regulation,[7] the gap is closing. Rising labor, transportation, and energy costs in other parts of the world, including China, have made offshore manufacturing significantly more expensive. When selling to the U.S. market, lower transportation costs are an advantage. Being closer to the customer can also be an advantage when design changes or production schedules need to be changed quickly. As a result of these factors, the Boston Consulting

---

7. Compared even to all nine of our largest trading partners.

Group estimates that China's overall manufacturing cost advantage has shrunk to just 4 percent. When labor productivity and the cost of shipping and inventory are included, it can be more economical to produce some products in the U.S. than in Asia.

In today's global environment, U.S. manufacturers must be nimble and creative. It helps if you are selling a better mousetrap. Companies with higher costs compensate by developing a value proposition. At our company, for instance, Clark-Reliance, we design and manufacture instrumentation devices for boilers, such as steam traps, controls, liquid level gages, and sight flow indicators. For the industries to which we sell -- oil and petro chemical and power generation, among others -- performance and safety are paramount. Our customers are more concerned with life cycle than with the initial expense. If, by choosing a less expensive alternative, our customers are going to go through two or three replacement parts in the same period that our product will continue to perform without replacement, ours is actually their least expensive option. That's also because a bad valve or control can waste hundreds of thousands of gallons of water or expensive chemicals in a single batch process. On some of our larger jobs, a repair person might have to climb three stories on a scaffold to be in a position to repair a boiler. In these instances, we need not under-price a competitor in China or India, as long as we are providing our clients with a superior product. Sometimes modern manufacturing is less about the process of turning raw materials into components or finished products, and more about a system designed to perform the activities required to deliver an end product that meets the customer's needs.

Some industries, of course, have a more difficult time than others creating a value proposition. It may be problematic for Ralph Lauren to demonstrate the value proposition between a $50 shirt manufactured in North Carolina and a $20 shirt made in Vietnam. That's why almost all clothing purchased in the United States is now imported. But there are plenty of other businesses which set themselves apart by using technical expertise to design a fundamentally better product. Long life, coupled with an ability to manufacture an item the first time with the correct design and performance, makes all the difference in the world to most clients. That is where small and midsize companies in the United States have an advantage if they have honed a value proposition based on the technical skills of their people.

Staying competitive in a global economy also means sourcing parts and components globally and managing global supply chains effectively. It means managing smart and understanding some key profit improvement principles. At its core, the goal of every effective business improvement philosophy is for the organization to perform better, faster, less expensive, more productive, and more profitable.

Competing in a "flat" world has forced U.S. manufacturers to adopt new management techniques, or rather, revisit old ones. In an environment filled with buzzwords, acronyms, and new names for old techniques, companies will do well to embrace some basic, proven profit improvement techniques that will never go out of style. Anyone can learn and implement them, and such practices can always be used to eliminate waste and improve quality. Explaining these methods so anyone can learn their magic is the goal of this book.

CHAPTER ONE

Gathering the Facts, Setting the Goals

There is nothing new except what has been forgotten.
Mademoiselle Bertin, hat maker to Marie Antoinette

Demystifying Six Sigma

Six Sigma may very well be the most popular management methodology in history. More than two hundred books have been written about it. A Google search turns up about eight million hits.

Six Sigma, as we know it today, began at Motorola in 1986 as a statistically-based method to reduce variation in electronic manufacturing processes. In its most literal iteration, Six Sigma performance is the statistical term for a process that produces fewer than 3.4 defects (or errors) per million opportunities. Its implementation includes black belts, sophisticated software, and rather obtuse acronyms like QFD,[8] TRIZ, [9] and SIPOC[10] diagrams.

Yet as Six Sigma has evolved, there has been less emphasis on its literal definition of counting defects in products and processes and more emphasis on its use to describe an overall business improvement methodology. It has come to mean many things because it is now interpreted in increasingly different ways, and is used as a moniker for almost any all-encompassing profit improvement program.

---

8. Quality Function Deployment (QFD) is described by Yoji Akao, who developed it in Japan in the 1960s, as a "method to transform user demands into design quality, to deploy the functions forming quality, and to deploy methods for achieving the design quality into subsystems and component parts, and ultimately to specific elements of the manufacturing process." (Akao, Yoji, 1994, "Development History of Quality Function Deployment")

9. Teoriya Resheniya Izobreatatelskikh Zadatch (Russian, translated as "Theory of Inventive Problem Solving")

10. Suppliers, Inputs, Process steps, Outputs, and Customers.

In other words, Six Sigma has become an ingenious way of branding and packaging all the different aspects of a comprehensive profit and quality improvement program.

Regardless of how broadly you define it, for it to work properly Six Sigma requires a foundation of tried and true methods that have proven successful for many decades.

DMAIC

The first stage in any Six Sigma-like or Total Quality Management process is to take a snapshot of your organization in order to provide a crystal clear picture of its financial health. Every profit improvement program needs to benchmark your company's performance in order to identify problems and set goals.

Six Sigma improvement programs use a method called DMAIC, an acronym that stands for define, measure, analyze, improve, and control. You can call it whatever you like, but the first three steps -- define, measure, and analyze – are the necessary initial steps of any profit improvement program. That's because before beginning any such program, the company president needs to understand where profits can be improved, and by how much. In our experience we have found that this can be accomplished quickly, without a multimillion dollar total Six Sigma effort. It doesn't require black belts, green belts, complicated mathematical formulas, or a substantial financial investment in consultants or manpower. In fact, these first steps can be conducted in 30 days, with information that should be readily accessible from your own financial manager.

Let's begin with defining, measuring and analyzing:
- Defining priorities and overall strategies,
- Measuring the efficiency of your organization, and
- Analyzing where your efforts can do the most good and how much profit improvement you can expect.

Our Sample Company

In this chapter we will use a small, fictional metal fabricating company to illustrate our message. Let's call it PIWB (Profit Improvement Without Bull) Inc.

Exhibit 1-1:
PIWB Inc., a $33.6 Million Company
with a 4% Pretax Profit of $1.344 million

Sales = $33.6 million

Material	40%
Direct Labor	7%
Overhead	16%
Cost of Sales	63%
Gross Margin	37%
Selling expenses	11%
Operating expenses[11]	22%
Total Operating Costs	33%
Pretax Profit	4% ($1.344 million)

PIWB Inc. has sales of $33.6 million and a 4 percent pretax profit of $1,344,000. In each chapter of this book our job will be to improve those numbers, but at this point cost of sales make up 63 percent of sales – 40 percent for materials, 7 percent for direct labor, and 16 percent for overhead, sometimes called burden. Overhead includes all manufacturing expenses, including indirect labor. Indirect labor is usually defined as any employee not directly related to adding value to the product being manufactured – people working in the warehouse, logistics, and maintenance, for example.

Our sample company's operating costs are 33 percent of sales – 11 percent for the sales department, which includes the regional and

11. Includes G&A and R&D expenses, commissions, and debt service.

executive sales managers and the inside sales group, and 22 percent for all other operating costs, which includes general and administrative and research and development costs, as well as interest and debt service, advertising, and marketing.

Your company, of course, will have its own breakdown, which may or may not be similar to PIWB's. The important point is that you should know these percentages from memory. If you aren't aware of where your company's money is being spent, you can't possibly know in what areas profit improvement will have the greatest impact.

The Growth Obsession

Before beginning any comprehensive profit improvement program, owners and managers of manufacturing companies must overcome their obsession with growth. If there is one thing we've learned during the past few decades as we have witnessed multiple corporate bankruptcies and other financial implosions, it is that a fixation on "more" is a sure prescription for disaster.

Using our example of a company doing $33.6 million in sales with a pretax profit of 4 percent, let's compare the impact of a 5 percent reduction in costs to a 5 percent increase in sales. The idea is to demonstrate that reducing costs is a far easier way to improve profits than increasing sales.

At this stage we've divided these costs only into the broad cost categories of material, direct labor, and selling and G & A (general and administrative). Look what happens if costs are reduced by just 5 percent overall, spread out among these categories. The savings go right to the bottom line, so now pretax profit has jumped from 4 percent to 9.5 percent, or from $1.344 million to $3.192 million. Pretax profit has more than doubled, just from a modest reduction in costs.

Exhibit 1-2:
$33.6 Million Manufacturing Company After
a 5% Reduction in Costs

Sales = $33.6 million

Material	38%
Direct Labor	7%
Overhead	15%
Cost of Sales	60%
Gross Margin	40%
Selling	9.5%
Operating expenses	21%
Total Operating Costs	30.5%
Pretax Profit	9.5% ($3.192 million)

Now imagine a 5 percent jump in sales, to $35.28 million. Assuming all other ratios stay the same, pretax profit would rise to $1.4112 million (4 percent of $35.28 million), just a 5 percent increase (1.4112 ÷ 1.344 = 1.05), compared to the more than 200 percent increase in our profit that we gained through a modest cost reduction effort.

And now, finally, ask yourself how much sales would have to increase in order to obtain the same doubling of pretax profits we gained through a 5 percent reduction in costs. You can see in Exhibit 1-3 that the answer is that sales need to more than double, from $33.6 million to a whopping $80 million. This is a truly remarkable jump even in the best economic times, and without the expense of acquiring another company or product line it is not realistic for most companies. To be sure, internal growth is part of a sound strategy (see Chapter 9). But it is unlikely to occur as quickly as reducing costs by just 5 percent.

Exhibit 1-3:
Sales Increase Necessary for a $33.6 Million Company with a 4% Profit Margin to Generate $3.192 Million Profit

Sales = $80 million

Material	40%
Direct Labor	7%
Overhead	<u>16%</u>
Cost of Sales	<u>63%</u>
Gross Margin	<u>37%</u>
Selling expenses	11%
Operating expenses	<u>22%</u>
Total Operating Costs	33%
Pretax Profit	4% ($3.2 million)

Growth is expensive. Sure, there are some savings during periods of growth, mainly from better absorption of fixed overhead and from economies of scale in the administrative and selling functions. But the savings derived from this kind of growth generally will not increase profit more than a percentage point, possibly two, and the strains on equipment and personnel will be substantial. Additional plant and equipment will likely be necessary to increase sales. There will also be a need for more working capital. The typical manufacturing company often requires working capital of 40-45 percent of sales, needed to pay for added inventory, obsolescence, accounts receivable, reserves, and interest charges. It usually also includes a small amount of operating cash.

Particularly during periods of high interest rates or tight credit, increased debt (which usually accompanies increased sales) can totally nullify your sales gain and can actually place you into a loss position. In contrast, with cost reduction, the savings and resulting profit improvement are immediate, dramatic, and inexpensive. That's why profit improvement techniques are so effective -- you don't have to find new working capital, increase debt or interest charges, hire new, inexperienced labor, or take on additional overhead to obtain added profits.

In other words, each added dollar in sales increase costs a company money, both in outlay and commitment of assets. Profit improvement through cost reduction does not.

Go Where the Money Is

Now let's make another few simple observations by taking another look at our $33.6 million company, with its original 4 percent pretax profit on sales of $1.2 million.

Exhibit 1-4:
$33.6 Million Company with a 4% Pretax
Profit of $1.344 million

Sales = $33.6 million

Material	40%
Direct Labor	7%
Overhead	16%
Cost of Sales	63%
Gross Margin	37%
Selling expenses	11%
Operating expenses	22%
Total Operating Costs	33%
Pretax Profit	4% ($1.344 million)

A glance at these numbers should immediately make clear where your profit improvement efforts should be concentrated. There are no hidden tricks. The logic is simple: tackle first those areas where the largest sums of money are involved, for this is where the greatest savings can be had. Put another way, concentrate your profit improvement efforts in the areas that impact profit the most.

An analysis of your own company's profit and loss statement may, of course, differ from the one outlined here. You may, for example, have other items to add to the list, such as research and development and debt service, which in this early example have been included in direct labor and overhead, respectively. But at manufacturing companies, material costs will almost certainly be your largest single expenditure as a percentage of sales, and direct labor one of the smallest.

Look at Exhibit 1-5. You can see that if we can get a 5 percent savings in material costs, we would get a 2.1 percent savings overall, which will go right to the bottom line. Compare this to a 1 percent savings from tackling overhead, and about a half of a percent savings from focusing on selling, G & A, or direct labor costs. With this in mind, in the exhibit below the third column lists the logical order of priority.

Exhibit 1-5:
Profit Improvement Priorities

Category	Percentage of Sales	Priority Number	Added Profit from 5% Reduction
Material	38%	Priority One	1.9 percent
Operating	21%	Priority Two	1 percent
Overhead	15%	Priority Three	.75 percent
Selling	9.5%	Priority Four	.475 percent
Labor	7%	Priority Five	.35 percent

Three Mistakes

Determining where the greatest savings can be realized, and therefore where you should concentrate your efforts, seems obvious. Yet in our experience most managers make three fundamental errors even before their profit improvement program gets underway.

In the first place, most U.S. business people have been trained to believe that sales growth should be their number one priority and they think they can grow to improve profits. We have just discussed why this is easier said than done. Remember, it took more than a 100 percent increase in sales to gain the same increase in pre-tax profits that we generated from just a 5 percent reduction in costs.

Secondly, U.S. managers become fixated on firing people --- on getting the short term rush of seeing their direct labor costs fall. If labor represents a large percentage of your company's total costs, by all means make it one of your profit improvement program's first priorities. But at manufacturing companies, there will almost certainly be far richer fields to harvest first. There is undoubtedly slippage in your direct labor, which we will address in Chapter 8, but the truth is, labor is the area where you will generally save the least, no matter how effective your program.

The third fundamental mistake made by many managers is making the purchase of new plants and equipment one of their initial profit improvement priorities. Chapter 8 will explain that while this indeed may reduce or eliminate some costs, it will also substantially increase overhead through interest and depreciation charges, and, if you are not careful, negate much, if not all, apparent savings.

Setting Goals

To initiate a comprehensive profit improvement program, today's Six Sigma-like methods often require a team of consultants to implement a program that will last six months or more in order to analyze every nook and cranny of your organization. If you have the financial resources to do this, by all means do it. Considerable benefits will surely result. Be prepared, however, to be inundated with all sorts of theories, and you had better quickly get up to speed on acronyms like ANOVA,[12] BPMN,[13] DPMO,[14] and RUMBA,[15] among many others.

12. ANOVA (analysis of variance) is an advanced method used to categorize and quantify the various sources of variation.

13. BPMN (business process modeling) has become a standard for modeling processes in statistical terms.

14. DPMO (defects per million opportunities) allows one to compare defect rates of products that have very different levels of complexity by measuring the defects per characteristic that could either result in a defect or a success.

15. RUMBA (reasonable, understandable, measurable, believable, attainable) is an acronym used in Six Sigma to help evaluate the appropriateness of any specification.

For most small and midsize companies, however, outside consultants will not be necessary in order to implement an effective profit improvement program. In fact, you should be able to analyze your own company's strengths and weaknesses and set long and short term goals within thirty days, with the assistance of only your chief financial officer.

Improving efficiencies, controlling costs, and maximizing profits will be the focus of most of this book. But for the moment, our job is to set some goals. How do you even know what's possible? If your $33.6 million company is making $1.344 million in pretax profits, what should be your goal? $2 million? $4 million? $6 million? $10 million? Once you set that goal, how should you get there?

A simple ratio analysis is our version of the first three steps of Six Sigma's DMAIC – to define the challenge, measure the past, and analyze the possibilities. We use a ratio analysis to understand our organization in a way that you otherwise would never be able to accomplish. And the idea is so simple. You just want to determine during which years your organization performed best in a variety of spending categories. Then you will make those best ratios your goal for the future. If you did it once, you should be able to do it again.

Exhibit 1-6:
Ratio Analysis Using a Five-Year History ($ in thousands)

COST OF SALES

	Sales $	Material $ %		Direct Labor $ %		Overhead[1] $ %		Selling[2] $ %	
YEAR 1	23,041	9,620	41.75	1,866	8.1	3,387	14.7	2,442	10.6
YEAR 2	27,923	10,890	39.0	2,290	8.2	3,518	12.6	3,675	13.16
YEAR 3	31,782	13,507	42.5	2,193	6.9	4,380	13.78	3,823	12.03
YEAR 4	29,223	11,454	39.2	2,108	7.2	5,328	18.2	2,913	9.95
YEAR 5	33,639	13,432	40	2,252	6.7	5,512	16.42	3,692	11.0
Best Ratios	$33,639	$13,119	39%	$2,254	6.7%	$4,239	12.6%	$3,347	9.95%

OPERATING EXPENSES

G & A[3] $ %		R&D[4] $ %		Commissions $ %		Debt Service $ %		Pretax Profit $ %	
2,318	10.06	256	1.11	1,588	6.89	576	2.5	988	4.29
3,164	11.33	360	1.29	2,077	7.44	810	2.9	1,139	4.08
3,064	9.64	385	1.21	2,222	6.99	667	2.1	1,541	4.85
2,930	10.01	357	1.22	1,660	5.67	907	3.1	1,516	5.18
3,823	11.39	480	1.43	1,947	5.58	1,208	3.6	1,366	4.07
$3,243	9.64%	$370	1.11%	$1,877	5.58%	$706	2.1%	$4,481	13.32%

[1] In this example, overhead (burden) costs include normal factory fixed and variable expenses, including indirect labor.
[2] In this example, selling costs include office overhead and advertising, as well as the regional and national sales forces.
[3] In this example, general and administrative costs include human resources, accounting, finance, the office of the president, and all other miscellaneous operating expenses.
[4] In this example, research and development includes R&D, but also quality control and engineering.

Ratio Analysis

Joseph Smith is the current President of PIWB Inc. He is frustrated because in looking at the most recent year's results, sales volume was at an all-time high, while profits were at an all-time low. No wonder he is concerned. Although sales during the past five years jumped more than 10 percent, from just over $23 million to an all-time high of $33.6 million, pretax profits fell from 4.29 percent to 4.07 percent. Your job is to find out why profits have drifted downward after a one-year spike in year four.

A simple ratio analysis of your total operation will identify the problem and allow you to target solutions. You can conduct this analysis in one weekend, in the comfort of your own home, returning to work Monday morning armed with the information you need to begin maximizing profits immediately. All you will need to begin is department figures for the previous five-year period (ten years is actually preferable). Ask your financial manager for the following figures for at least the past five years, both in dollar amounts and as a percentage of sales.

- Sales volume
- Material, labor, and overhead costs
- Selling costs, including commissions
- General and administrative (G&A) costs
- Research and development (R&D) expenditures
- Debt service costs
- Pretax profits

Don't be surprised if you start hearing all sorts of reasons and excuses as to why these numbers are not readily available. You may be told that your company does not break them down into these same categories, or that multiple changes in accounting procedures have taken place over the years, making a comparison between apples and apples impossible. Don't believe any of it. Of course, your company's categories may not be identical to what you see in Exhibit 1-6. But your chief financial officer should be able to compare costs over at least a five-year period in broad categories such as labor, material, and selling.

There is an added benefit in asking for these numbers. Just the request alone will provide an excellent opportunity for you to evaluate your accounting department and to gain a thorough appraisal and understanding of your financial manager and your accounting procedures. If these numbers are unavailable, there is something wrong, and changes need to be made immediately in order to force feed the availability of this kind of data into your normal way of doing business. You will also learn something seeing the way these numbers are assembled. By becoming familiar with your financial manager's techniques and methods, you will make certain that your company's accounting procedures are standardized, up-to-date, and readily accessible.

In assembling these figures, your purpose is to determine the lowest ratio of cost as a percentage of sales for each of the operational categories. In which year did the expenditures in each category impose the least drain on profitability? If your operation is typical, you will find that all the best ratios did not occur in the same year. Sales were a factor, of course, but your five-year profile will undoubtedly show that gross profits were best in one year, G & A was lowest in another, selling costs were the least percentage of sales in yet another year, and so on.

Stare at Exhibit 1-6 and several questions should jump out at you. Notice that selling costs were substantially less in year four than any other year. Specific steps to improve efficiencies in the selling functions will be discussed shortly, but there are some obvious steps you can take immediately. Ask your sales force for their opinions. Provide them the numbers and ask for their ideas as to what the company might have been doing differently in year four. Were they short staffed that year? Over-staffed? Was there a particular salesperson who had a good year but who now is no longer with the company? Your people will probably have other ideas that do not occur to you or your direct reports.

Ask other departments the same types of questions, but also turn the scrutiny on yourself. Why, for example, in the most recent year might there have been such a big jump in general and administrative costs as a percentage of sales? Did that include your own executive staff and expenses?

Also think carefully about any trends that may be having an impact on material costs, since that is your largest single cost category. In our example the cost of materials as a percentage of sales seems to be all over the place, down one year and up the next. We will see in Chapters 3 and 4 that developing an efficient, cost-conscious purchasing department reporting directly to the chief executive officer is the most important single task of any comprehensive profit improvement effort.

At some point you will also want to look at debt service, since it is not a good sign if the cost of servicing your debt has been creeping upwards. This is likely due to variances in working capital requirements. As for R&D, there is no need to be too concerned with these percentage increases as displayed in Exhibit 1-6, since a small increase in R&D is not necessarily a bad thing, particularly if increased sales have meant increased profits. In most cases, R&D should not be cut as a way to improve the bottom line. In fact, once you start to see profit improvement from the steps you will be taking, we encourage managers to put some of that savings into productive R & D projects.

Comparing Your Company with Others

After studying a ratio analysis of your company, compare your bottom line figures with those of other companies in the same industry and in the same sales bracket. Depending on your category, this data can be gathered from companies like Beacon Equity Research, the Dunn & Bradstreet company, or Hoover's. You can also download the 10K files and annual reports of publicly held companies from the SEC's EDGAR database. Look for companies that are in your type of business and are of comparable size. Have your financial manager translate these numbers so you can easily compare them to each category in your own company's operations. In which areas are you more efficient than your competition? In which areas does it look like you could use the most improvement?

The Best That We Can Be

Now let's look at our ratio analysis as a way to determine the profit that would be attainable by using the most favorable ratios during each of the five years of operations. Note that these ratios have been highlighted in red and brought down to the bottom line in Exhibit 1-6, so our ideal company looks like this:

Exhibit 1-7:
Pre-Tax Profit Using Best Ratios

Sales = $33,639,000

	Best Ratio (%)	From Year
Material	39.0	Two
Labor	6.7	Five
Overhead	12.6	Two
Selling	9.95	Four
G & A	9.64	Three
R&D	1.11	One
Commissions	5.58	Five
Debt service	2.1	Three
	84.68	
Pretax Profit	15.32	

Our ratio analysis shows that pretax profits ranged from a low of 4.07 percent in year five, to a high of 5.18 percent in year four. But by accumulating the best ratios into one ideal year, we see that a pretax profit of about 15.3 percent is actually attainable. Now we have something to shoot for.

In the chapters to come we will set our sights on matching or bettering the best ratios we have ever achieved in each category. We will work to make material costs no more than 39 percent of sales, overhead no more than 12.6 percent, selling and G&A no more than 10 percent, and labor less than 7.2 percent. Remember, these percentages are unique to PIWB Inc. Because of the nature of your particular business, your material or labor costs might be higher, or lower. But a ratio analysis will allow you to set your own goals.

This ratio analysis can be considered a macro analysis, since it is intended to provide you with an accurate perspective on your total operations. A micro ratio analyses of individual departments and operations -- of the various costs associated with the purchasing function, for example -- can sharpen your focus further. The idea is to continually and constantly identify profit improvement goals, then use the techniques laid out in subsequent chapters to meet those goals.

Summary

So what have we learned?

- We've learned that comprehensive profit improvement programs like Six Sigma and Lean Manufacturing require a foundation of tried and true methods that have proven successful for many decades.
- We've learned that eliminating waste is a much easier, more efficient way to improve profits than increasing sales.
- We've learned that it is best to concentrate your profit improvement efforts on those areas where you are spending most of your company's dollars.
- And we've learned that a simple ratio analysis will reveal how profits can be increased substantially just by mimicking your company's best efficiencies from previous years.

CHAPTER TWO

Use Your Head During the First Week and for the Rest of Your Life

Take a look again at the macro ratio analysis in the previous chapter displayed in Exhibit 1-6. These are numbers that your financial manager or chief financial officer can hand you on a Friday. By Monday morning you should be ready to share some very specific goals with your key personnel. You can, for example, tell your head of purchasing that the goal of that department will be to achieve results that are obviously obtainable, since they were already achieved three years earlier -- namely material costs of 39 percent of sales. Likewise, you can tell your sales and departmental managers that they will be responsible for maintaining selling and general and administrative costs at 9.95 percent and 9.64 percent of sales, respectively. And you can challenge your financial manager to come up with ways to keep overhead less than 12.6 percent. They did it before, they can do it again.

Ratio Analysis of Selling Costs

In the previous chapter we conducted a ratio analysis of the entire company for the past five years. We learned that if you combine the best ratios of each year and move them into a single year, your company's pretax profits will jump by almost 300 percent. As you look at these numbers, you might begin to wonder what was done right in year two, when material costs were only 39 percent of sales and overhead was only 12.6 percent, or year three when general and administrative expenses were only 9.64 percent of sales, or year four when selling costs were less than 10 percent for the only time during the five-year period.

During this first weekend of profit improvement review, your macro analysis should have provided you with an accurate perspective on the total operations of your company. Now it is time to take a look at specific categories in order to determine *why* certain costs have remained in line, and why others have been increasing as a percentage of sales. This can only be accomplished through a more detailed, in-depth probe, which will reward you with the specifics (also culled from five- or ten-year data) for each separate category. This will sharpen your focus to the point where you can readily determine the profit improvement measures that will benefit your operations the most.

Ordinarily, you would conduct your microanalysis, as well as all profit improvement efforts, in descending order of categories, starting with those involving the most dollars. (See exhibit 1-5.) For now, however, we are going to concentrate on selling costs. Ask your financial manager for a breakdown of selling costs for the last five (or ten) years so that you can look at them on a lowest cost basis, just as you did for general operations. Exhibit 2-1 breaks down selling costs for PIWB Inc., which, in this example, has sales during this five-year period of between just over $23 million to $37 million. Remember, the specific categories for your own company will undoubtedly be different. Depending on the nature of your business, for example, you may also want to itemize commissions, advertising, telephone, warehouse rent and taxes, office supplies, postage, depreciation, and insurance. Regardless, the goal is to determine the lowest cost as a percentage of sales in every category you can quantify.

Exhibit 2-1:
Ratio Analysis in the Selling Expense Area

	Year One		Year Two		Year Three		Year Four		Year Five			Lowest Cost/Ratio
	$	% to NS	$	% to NS	$	% to NS	$	% to NS	$	% to NS	$	% to NS
Net Sales	23,041,000	100	27,872,000	100	31,782,000	100	35,244,000	100	37,000,000	100		100
Selling Home Office												
Salaries, Wages, etc.	471,002	2.04	478,864	1.72	486,745	1.53	649,821	1.84	753,962	2.04		1.53
Fringe Benefits	19,102	.08	32,470	.12	53,043	.17	64,025	.18	94,861	.26		.08
Travel and Entertainment	84,291	.37	102,785	.37	43,002	.45	157,469	.45	155,820	.42		.37
Sales Meetings & Conventions	54,009	.23	80,967	.29	82,233	.26	93,182	.27	103,842	.28		.23
Other	208,853	.91	193,291	.69	248,186	.78	394,928	1.12	388,386	1.05		.69
Total	837,257	3.63	888,377	3.19	1,013249	3.19	1,359,425	3.86	1,498,872	4.05	1,073,000	2.90
Branch Expense												
Supervisors	136,784	.59	141,120	.51	175,043	.55	202,489	.57	215,567	.58		.51
Salespeople's salaries and commissions	556,434	2.46	647,788	2.32	706,897	2.23	782,903	2.22	805,891	2.18		2.18

	$	% to NS	$	% to NS	$	% to NS	$	% to NS	$	% to NS	Lowest Cost/Ratio % to NS
Stockhandlers	184,271	.80	235,768	.84	296,977	.93	353,784	1.00	311,972	.85	.80
Other Wages	109,398	.48	110,708	.40	149,904	.47	159,571	.45	115,478	.31	.31
Fringe Benefits	63,129	.27	108,988	.27	144,249	.38	179,938	.45	190,587	.52	.27
FixedExpenses	299,510	1.30	361,273	1.30	398,387	1.25	386,133	1.10	444,061	1.20	1.10
Travel and Entertainment	184,916	.80	197,473	.80	215,184	.68	215,414	.61	266,360	.72	.61
Freight	184,430	.80	229,265	.82	297,666	.94	301,651	.86	278,000	.75	.75
Other	181,622	.79	186,454	.67	244,669	.77	249,346	.71	234,090	.63	.63
Total	1,910,494	8.29	2,216,837	7.95	2,628,976	8.27	2,831,229	8.03	2,862,004	7.74	7.16
Outlying Plants	20,627	.09	21,439	.08	24,862	.08	34,712	.10	31,152	.08	.08
Advertising	600,220	2.61	682,150	2.45	849,493	2.45	936,295	2.65	900,000	2.43	2.43
Grand Total	3,368,598	14.62	3,808,803	13.67	4,538,874	14.28	5,161,861	14.64	5,348,849	14.45	12.57
# of Ratios Used	5		4		2		2		6		

Note that salaries and wages in the home office had their lowest ratio to net sales in year three, at 1.53 percent. The other most favorable ratios are:

- Fringe benefits -- .08 percent
- Travel and expenses -- .37 percent
- Sales meetings and conventions -- .23 percent
- Other expenses and costs -- .69 percent

For branch office costs, the best ratios were:

- Supervisors -- .51 percent
- Salespeople's salaries and commissions -- 2.18 percent
- Stockhandlers -- .80 percent
- Other wages -- .31 percent
- Fringe benefits -- .27 percent
- Fixed expenses -- 1.10 percent
- Travel and entertainment -- .61 percent
- Freight -- .75 percent
- Other expenses -- .63 percent
- Outlying plants -- .08 percent
- Advertising -- 2.43 percent

In Exhibit 2-1, all these figures have been brought down to the last row in order to come up with a ratio of total selling costs to total sales. The most favorable ratio, 13.67 percent, occurred in year two, but the company's sales department had successes in other years as well. If you count the shaded figures, you will see that it had five of its best ratios in the first year, four in the second, two in the third, and six in the fifth. Remember, in the previous chapter we showed the significant profit improvement that could occur if all the best ratios were achieved in the same year. Now we've done the same for selling costs. The most favorable ratios in each category have been brought over to the final column. You can see that if the company had achieved all its best ratios in the same year, total selling costs would have been 12.57 percent. You've shaved off 1.1 percent from the best the company had ever achieved – 13.67 percent in year two. At a company with $37 million in sales, that's almost a $700,000 profit improvement that goes right to the bottom line. You have to use your common sense to determine if there were special circumstances that explained the results in any one year. Was there a catastrophic fire that increased costs in one of those years? Did the company hire an expensive, if very effective, salesperson at the beginning of year four?

Ratio Analysis of Other Departmental Areas

In order to improve your return on sales by another several percentage points, a micro ratio analysis also can be applied to other broad categories, like overhead, G & A, and even to the purchasing department. Because of price fluctuations beyond your control, the cost of materials does not lend itself particularly well to a ratio analysis. But other purchasing costs, such as personnel and overhead, *can* be broken down in this way in order to pinpoint areas of potential profit improvement.

Ratio analysis certainly should be applied to overhead, which can represent up to 20 percent of all costs. In Exhibit 2-3, the overhead costs of a typical manufacturing company have been broken down. Again, the lowest percentage for each item is highlighted. Notice the steady upward creep of the overall overhead percentage. What should your target be for year six? Where can the greatest savings be realized? One number that should jump out at you is the cost of indirect labor, which has increased at a greater rate than most other items.

Exhibit 2-2:
Micro Ratio Analysis of Overhead Costs

(% of Sales Dollar)

Overhead Expenses	Year One	Year Two	Year Three	Year Four	Year Five	Best Ratios
Salaries	3.5	3.2	3.5	3.6	3.6	3.2
Benefits	.6	.4	.7	.8	1.0	.4
Indirect Labor	3.7	4.1	5.1	5.6	5.9	4.1
Hourly Benefits	2.2	3.2	3.1	3.8	3.6	2.2
Supplies	1.2	1.4	1.2	1.2	1.2	1.2
Maintaining Parts/Tools	.9	1.2	.8	.9	1.0	.8
Utilities	.6	.8	.6	.8	.7	.6
Depreciations	1.2	2.5	1.8	1.6	1.6	1.2
Taxes	.5	.7	.5	.5	.5	.5
Insurance	.2	.2	.3	.3	.4	.2
Leased Building	1.4	1.1	1.2	1.2	.9	.9
Equipment Rental	.1	.2	.1	.2	.2	.1
Miscellaneous	.5	.3	.5	.8	.7	.3
TOTAL	16.0	19.1	18.6	21.1	19.9	15.7

Note that by using the best ratios for each year, we have lowered overhead costs to 15.7 percent of sales, shaving 4.2 percentage points off of the company's current overhead costs. At the same $37 million company, that's another $1.5 million that goes straight to the bottom line.

Constant Dollar per Employee
Another simple yet extremely useful way to measure the health of a company is to track the constant dollar sales per employee. This should be conducted at the same time as ratio analysis and, like ratio analysis, it can almost instantly provide you with some valuable information about your company. It can offer you a quick but revealing window into worker productivity and suggest to you the status of overall management efficiency.

Exhibit 2-3: Constant Dollar Sales Per Employee

Sales Per Employee
(in $s)

	Year 1	Year 2	Year 3	Year 4	Year 5	Year 6
Salaried – Exempt	38	38	36	34	39	45
Salaried – Nonexempt	28	30	25	33	31	33
Hourly – Direct	77	83	79	76	96	108
Hourly – Indirect	28	37	38	51	42	42
Total Employees	171	188	178	194	208	228
OT (Overtime) Equivalents (included above)						
Salaried	0	1	1	1	1	1
Hourly	6	8	3	10	9	9
Total OT Equivalents	6	9	4	11	10	10
Net Sales (in millions)	$29	30	31	33	35	37
Constant Dollar Sales (CDS)[16] (in millions)	$33.62	33.77	33.87	35.01	36.05	37
CDS/Total Employees	$196,608	179,628	190,280	180,463	173,317	162,280

Study Exhibit 2-3. Immediately you can determine that although this company has increased its sales steadily during the most recent five-year period -- from $29 million to $37 million -- and although the

16. Adjusted for inflation at an average annual inflation rate of 3%

number of employees has increased by only 30 percent, the real story is told when constant dollar figures are scrutinized. Constant dollar sales per employee have actually decreased from almost $200,000 to just over $162,000.

Note also that the best ratio of constant dollar sales to employee was obtained in year one and almost peaked again in year three, before dropping off rather sharply. What does this drop-off mean in real terms? By dividing the constant dollar sales for the most recent year (year six - $37 million) by the constant dollar sales for the best year (year one - $33.62 million), note that, after adjusting for a modest average annual rate of 3 percent inflation[17], sales have had a real growth of 10 percent (37 million ÷ 33.62 million = 1.1). The number of employees, therefore, should not have increased by more than 10 percent. Note that:

- Salaried exempt employees should have numbered 42 rather than 45.
- Salaried nonexempt employees should have numbered 31 rather than 33.
- Hourly direct employees should have numbered 84, rather than 108.
- Hourly indirect employees should have numbered 31, rather than 42.

This company, therefore, has approximately 40 employees too many. By adding workers according to the actual sales dollars rather than constant dollars, and by allowing "personnel creep" to enter into the organization over time, this company ended up with an unnecessary employee surplus of almost 20 percent. Remember, this assumes that in year one, the four categories of personnel were fully efficient. There actually is no reason to make that assumption. In fact, to the

---

17. This is a reasonable estimate. The overall inflation rate may have averaged much less than 3 percent annually for the past five years, but certain prices, like for oil and other commodities, have likely increased much more than that. Using a higher rate of inflation would only increase the number of excess employees in this example.

extent the company was inefficient in year one, the problem of excess costs due to excess personnel is further compounded.

Exhibit 2-4:
Personnel Creep from Constant Dollar Graph

	Year One	Year Six Target*	Year Six Actual	Difference btw. Target and Actual
Salaried-Exempt	38	38 x 109% = 42	45	3
Salaried-Nonexempt	28	28 x 109% = 31	33	2
Hourly-Direct	77	77 x 109% = 84	108	24
Hourly-Indirect	28	28 x 109% = 31	42	11
Total Employees	171	188	228	40

*Rounded up

It should be noted that, depending on a variety of factors -- including type of business -- companies will vary widely as to their sales per employee. The company charted in Exhibit 2-4 and 2-5 happens to have between $160,000 and $200,000 in sales per employee, but we know companies that are getting less than $100,000 and more than $250,000 in constant dollar sales and are doing just fine. Regardless of where a company falls in the spectrum, the goal should be to increase the ratio.

Organizational Analysis

There is one other simple, yet extremely effective, technique you can use to immediately get started on the path toward maximizing profits. In this case, the only reference material you will need is an accurate, up-to-date organization chart that includes the salary of each employee. As chief executive, you should already know your own organizational structure, both in the shop and in sales. Salaries, travel expenses, and fringes can be furnished by accounting personnel.

The object of an organizational analysis is to determine how company departments can be streamlined and reorganized in such a way as to not only cut costs, but also increase effectiveness and productivity. You can do the restructuring on a yellow pad while you relax with a cup of coffee. It may be, for example, that some of your managers have too much responsibility, while others don't have enough. Or perhaps those responsible for committing the bulk of your company's money are too isolated from the top executive responsible for the company's bottom line performance.

No one in your entire salaried organization should be overlooked in an organizational analysis -- from the chief executive, down through the foremen, to each department, to the most junior person on the sales force. At first, this may seem like an impossible assignment. But regardless of the company's size, you will see that an organizational analysis can successfully be conducted for the entire company, for each profit center, and for your own reporting structure.

Three Rules

Before taking a look at your own organizational chart or the sample charts presented in this chapter, begin by recognizing three very basic, but often broken, organizational rules:

1. Follow the 7-10 span-of-control rule. An executive should supervise no more than ten employees, but no less than seven.
2. Make sure the chief executive is supervising those who spend the bulk of the company's money. The executives responsible for the departments that can most affect profits should report directly to the head of the company.
3. Don't insulate management. Without breaking the first rule, the number of management levels between the company head and the lowest level of supervision should be kept to an absolute minimum.

These rules may seem simple, and they are. But in many corporations they are ignored or forgotten, resulting in a bloated, inefficient organizational structure that shields you from what is really going on in the company.

Take our 7-10 span-of-control rule. Every executive should directly supervise no more than ten persons, and no less than seven. With fewer than seven, executives will not be fully utilizing their time or abilities; with more than ten, they will usually be spreading themselves too thin. There are exceptions, of course. On the manufacturing floor, for example, one foreman can maintain control of up to fifteen persons in a complicated operation, and up to fifty or more in a simple operation. But for most executives, between 7 and 10 is the optimum number.

In tandem with the 7-10 rule, as chief executive you also want to have direct control over the departments that influence profits the most. That means that the 7-10 executives who report directly to the CEO should almost always include the financial manager and the directors of the sales, manufacturing, supply chain management, human resources, and engineering departments. This still leaves between one and four positions open, to be tailored to your own specific operation. These guidelines assume, of course, a profit center operation as opposed to a corporate headquarters of a multi-division company.

The person who is probably most often left off this list is the one person who should virtually always report directly to the chief executive of any manufacturing company: the purchasing director. As will be discussed in detail in the next chapter, the director of purchasing often controls as much as 50 percent of the sales dollar, and therefore has a substantial impact on a company's bottom line performance. Many companies nevertheless allow the purchasing chief to report to the plant manager (or even to the assistant plant manager), or to a materials manager, who in turn might report to someone below the level of president. Other times, purchasing is mistakenly put under manufacturing, or combined with inventory and production control. All these mistakes isolate a key department from the chief executive.

The head of industrial relations, or human resources, is another executive who should almost always report directly to the chief executive officer. Human resources no longer merely involves hiring the right people and keeping them happy and productive. It involves insurance, compensation, retirement benefits, labor negotiations, personnel, equal opportunity, safety, and a host of other costly functions, including budget-gobbling fringe benefits, which can total up to 40 percent of your salary and wage costs.

Exhibit 2-5 Current Manufacturing Organization

Co./Division President

Director of Manufacturing
$110,000

Production Control
$70,000

Plant Manager
$75,000

Purchasing
$80,000

Industrial Engineering
$60,000

Quality Control
$70,000

Industrial Relations
$70,000

General Superintendent
$60,000

General Foreman, Fabrication
$55,000

General Foreman, Assembly
$55,000

Foreman, Machining, Dept. 1
$50,000
20 people

Foreman, Machining, Dept. 2
$50,000
25 people

Foreman, Machining, Dept. 3
$50,000
15 people

Foreman, Heavy Assembly, Dept. 4
$50,000
19 people

Foreman, Heavy Assembly, Dept. 5
$50,000
12 people

Foreman, Heavy Assembly, Dept. 6
$50,000
25 people

Foreman, Heavy Assembly, Dept. 7
$50,000
12 people

Total Salaries = $1,055,000

As a first step toward reorganizing your own company, study Exhibit 2-5, the organizational chart for a fictional metals fabricating company's manufacturing department. Consider how you would make your organization more effective and responsive by streamlining it and eliminating the excess. As you begin, be certain to keep in mind the three rules discussed earlier. Seek to cut the level of reporting, make certain that the proper departments report to the proper people, and at the same time determine how personnel logically and effectively can be consolidated.

After studying Exhibit 2.5, you will note, for example, that there is a director of manufacturing making $110,000 to whom only three department heads report directly. One of these is the head of the purchasing department. Ask yourself if this is a good arrangement.

There is a plant manager earning $75,000, to whom the industrial engineering, quality control, and human resources departments report. There is a general superintendent earning $60,000, and two general foremen, one in charge of fabrication, the other in charge of assembly. They each make $55,000. Is there a way to consolidate these positions?

There are seven foremen, all of whom are five reporting levels away from the president. They each earn $50,000, and supervise between 12 and 25 people:

- The foreman in charge of the machine shop supervises 20 people.
- The foreman in charge of the press department supervises 25 people.
- The welding foreman employs 15 people.
- The foreman of heavy assembly supervises 19 people.
- One light assembly foreman has 12 people under him.
- The other light assembly foreman has 25 people.
- The foreman of shipping and receiving supervises 12 people.

From these figures, we can estimate that this company is doing anywhere between $10 million and $30 million in sales. In just about this same form, thousands of companies exist throughout the United States and in many other industrialized countries. In most cases, these companies grow and mature without ever losing their baby fat, until drastic remedial measures are suddenly necessary.

Try your hand at restructuring this typical organization from the top down. Re-diagram it on paper according to your new specifications. Approach the assignment in at least five ways:

1. Raise the reporting level of key departments to as high a level as possible, consistent with the importance of their respective functions.
2. Rearrange reporting relationships so that related departments report to the proper people.
3. Eliminate underutilized personnel and consolidate departments where feasible.
4. Minimize the number of management reporting levels.
5. Make your final adjustments based on the strengths and weaknesses of the people comprising your particular organization.

Chances are even at first glance, opportunities for immediate improvements will be apparent. Can you streamline operations, eliminating or consolidating employee positions? Are any departments reporting to the wrong people? Can any of the manufacturing departments be consolidated?

After you have tried your own skills at streamlining the organization, estimate how much you have saved in salaries and fringes. What percentage is this of a $10, $20, or $30 million dollar operation?

Exhibit 2-6 offers one way an effective reorganization could be accomplished. Bear in mind that there is no single "right" way to reorganize this department. If you didn't come up with the same reorganization plan as the one outlined in Exhibit 2-6, yours is not necessarily wrong, only different. Always adjust your organization plan according to your people and their abilities. Do not try to fit a square peg into a round hole.

Your goals should remain constant, however. You want to save salary costs where you can, but much more important is to establish a

Exhibit 2-6: Revised Manufacturing Organization

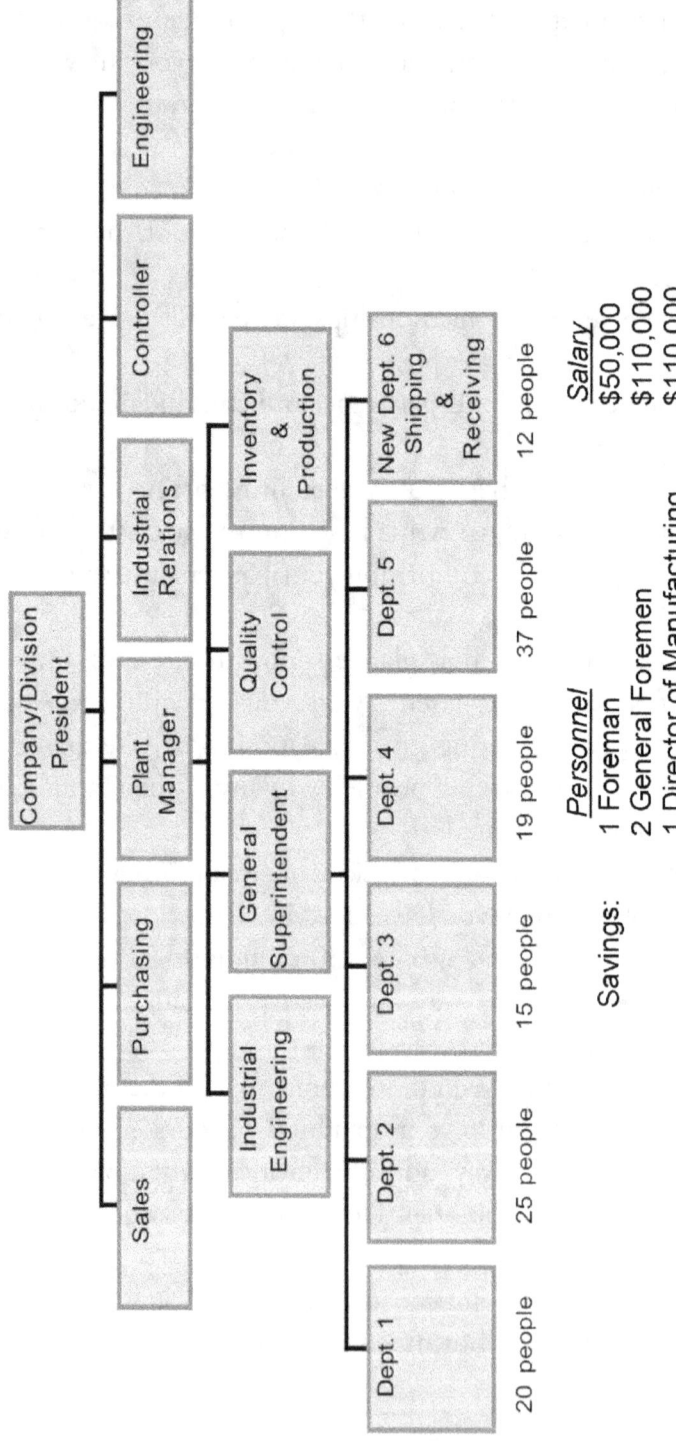

Total organizational savings*: $270,000 or 2.7% in a $10 million company
1.8% in a $15 million company
1.35% in a $20 million company

hierarchy that will allow you to efficiently control costs and maximize profits. You will note that in our reorganization, by eliminating the director of manufacturing ($110,000 a year) an entire bureaucratic level has been excised. The reorganization has also eliminated two general foremen for a savings of another $110,000 a year, and one foreman (light assembly) for an additional savings of $50,000. Retained are the plant manager and the general superintendent. Also intact are the machine shop, press, welding, and heavy assembly departments. But the two light assembly departments have been combined.

In the old organization (Exhibit 2-5), only one person, the director of manufacturing, reported directly to the president. This violated all three of our rules simultaneously. One direct report is not enough for the top executive. Even if the plant manager and head of production control and purchasing were added, these four still would not meet our span-of-control rules. Some of the key elements of the organization will still be unnecessarily removed from your supervision. There are simply too many levels for the chief executive to have a good feel for the strengths and weaknesses of the total organization.

In the revised organization (Exhibit 2-6), we have placed the president two levels closer to the departments related to manufacturing. The president could even supervise three or four more areas if the size or nature of this particular business demanded it. For example, quality control could report directly to the president if it were a particularly important department, or if it would be compromised by reporting to the plant manager.

Under the revised plan, the plant manager will have direct responsibility for the general superintendent, industrial engineering, quality control, and inventory and production control. This still gives the plant manager the opportunity to fulfill other tasks, which is why some people would say he or she should also handle purchasing. But, as we will hammer home throughout this book, purchasing is generally where the bulk of a manufacturing company's money is spent. Consequently, the purchasing head should always report directly to the president when material represents a large percentage of the sales dollar.

Note that in the original organizational structure there was no category for inventory control, a most essential function, without which effective material cost control will be almost impossible. We have created a department head for inventory and production control who reports directly to the plant manager. (Under the old organization, the head of production control reported to the director of manufacturing.)

The general foremen for both fabrication and assembly have been eliminated, since using the 7-10 span-of-control rule, they were underutilized under the old organization. The seven foremen under them have also been consolidated. Remember, our rule concerning span of control differentiates between the number of persons a foreman can supervise in a complicated operation (such as machining or heavy assembly), and a simple operation (light assembly). In the revised organizational chart we have, therefore, combined departments 5 and 6 so that one foreman supervises 37 people in the light assembly operation, but that the foreman in the heavy assembly operation has no more than 19 people. Machining, which remains a separate department with 20 persons, is a skilled, or "difficult," operation.

We could also make a case that the plant manager should be eliminated, which would allow the next level to report directly to the president. The president's span of control would then be nine, still within our range. The same argument could be made for eliminating the general superintendent, but keeping the plant manager. Either change would provoke additional savings, but would be a jolt to any organization. Unless your company is in serious financial difficulty and dramatic changes need to be made immediately, in our judgment we have done enough for now. We would suggest allowing your changes time to settle in before considering further alternatives during the next organizational analysis, which should be conducted six months or a year down the road.

What, then, in addition to improving efficiencies, have we accomplished during our weekend of work at home in terms of real, immediate savings from a simple restructuring of our organizational chart?

- We saved the salary of the director of manufacturing, amounting to $110,000.
- We saved the salaries of two general foremen (fabrication and assembly), for a total of another $110,000.
- We saved the salary of one foreman of light assembly, amounting to $50,000.

The total savings is $270,000, representing 2.7 percent of a company doing $10 million in sales, 1.8 percent of a company doing $15 million in sales, and 1.35 percent for a $20 million company. We also saved 25 percent of the line manufacturing supervisory costs ($270,000 savings divided by total salary costs of $1,055,000), and that does not even include the savings to be realized in fringe benefits, which can be 40 percent or more of salary costs.

Not only have we cut costs, we have also minimized the number of levels between top management and first line executives. Decreasing the levels of supervision should increase communication, productivity, and effectiveness. The goal is to streamline the organization, connecting the top executive to all of the most important reporting departments, so that you are in direct control of all the key profit areas. With better control over key areas, the top executive will have more control over the total operation.

In summary, aim for a reorganization that will save at least 1-2 percent of sales. If you get more, you're fortunate; if you get less, question your techniques.

We have just witnessed how organizational analysis can create immediate and substantial savings. "Personnel creep" will always occur at all levels of an organization unless you, as the top executive, remain diligent about preventing it. We once visited a foundry that had had relatively flat sales during the previous three years, but a simple organizational analysis revealed that the number of pattern makers had jumped from three to eleven. The president of one company we were looking to acquire had 23 people reporting directly to him. No wonder he had no time to take the steps necessary to improve profits.

Organizational Analysis of Sales Department
Just like ratio analysis, once the technique of organizational analysis is mastered, it can be repeated for every department. Let's again use the sales department as an example.

Direct your attention to Exhibit 2-7, which outlines PIWB Inc.'s sales organization. Note that this selling organization has three top executives: a general sales manager, an Eastern regional sales manager, and a Western regional sales manager. Reporting to them are:

- A New England district sales manager with four salespeople producing sales of $2.4 million, averaging $600,000 per salesperson.
- A Southeastern district sales manager with three salespeople producing $2.4 million in sales, averaging $800,000 per salesperson.
- An East Central district manager with six salespeople producing $5 million, averaging nearly $834,000 per salesperson.
- A Southern district manager, with four salespeople producing $2 million, in sales, averaging $500,000 per salesperson.
- A Midwestern district manager, with six salespeople producing $4.2 million in sales, averaging $700,000 per salesperson.
- A Southwestern district manager, with two salespeople producing $600,000 in sales, averaging $300,000 per salesperson.
- A Western district manager, with four salespeople producing $1.6 million in sales, averaging $400,000 per salesperson.

The cast of characters: three generals, seven colonels, and twenty-nine privates, producing sales of $18.2 million. That seems like a substantial army for so small of a company. Let's take a look.

Exhibit 2-7: Current Sales Organization

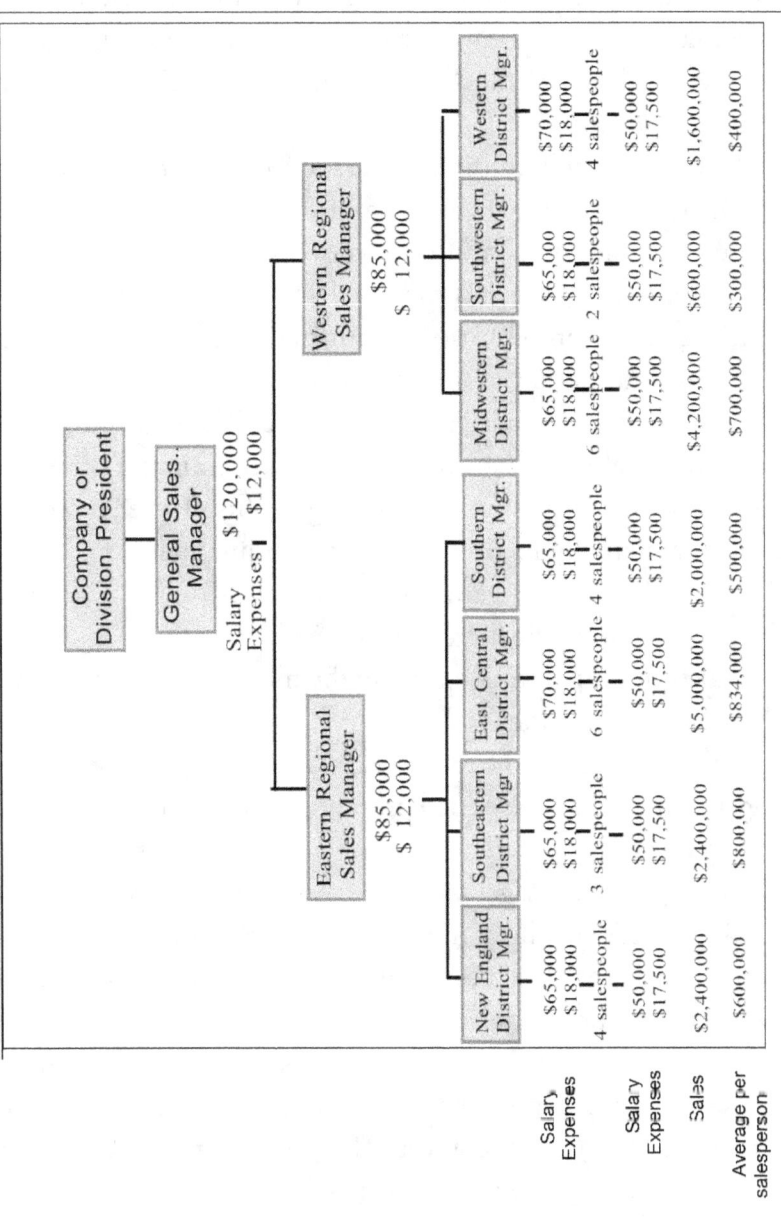

Total Salaries and Expenses = $1,389,500

At a glance you can see that there is an imbalance. Take a look at the sales per salesperson in each district. A comparison between the Southwestern and East Central district shows a serious inequity. Salespeople in the Southwestern district are averaging $300,000 apiece, while those in the East Central average $834,000, almost 300 percent greater.

Before turning to Exhibit 2-8, the revised sales organization chart, take a pencil and a piece of paper and try to work out a reorganization you might apply to your own sales operation. Bear in mind the rules for span of control and the reporting relationships that we discussed in connection with the reorganization of the manufacturing organization. And again, don't be discouraged if your reorganization does not match the model illustrated here. There are no absolutes in organizational analysis – or, for that matter, in any other of our foundational techniques for maximizing profits. There are only basic rules, fundamental guidelines, and personal judgments.

In the revised sales organization (Exhibit 2-8), you will note that we have made some drastic changes. We have implemented a thorough shakeup, simply from studying the inconsistencies and waste in the original organization.

We have eliminated the two regional managers. With seven district managers out in the field, there hardly seems to be any justification for costly regional managers. If this company is representative of a great many, the regional manager's job is a reward to people who have done something special for the company or who have put in many years of work, perhaps when the company was starting up or initiating growth.

We have reduced the number of district sales managers from seven to five. We have combined the Southern and Southeastern districts, and have eliminated the Southwestern district by making it part of the Western operation. The New England, East Central, and Midwestern districts have been left intact. Even now, all five district managers, and especially the individuals responsible for New England and Western districts, could actually supervise more salespeople. They therefore have room to grow.

Exhibit 2-8 Revised Sales Organization

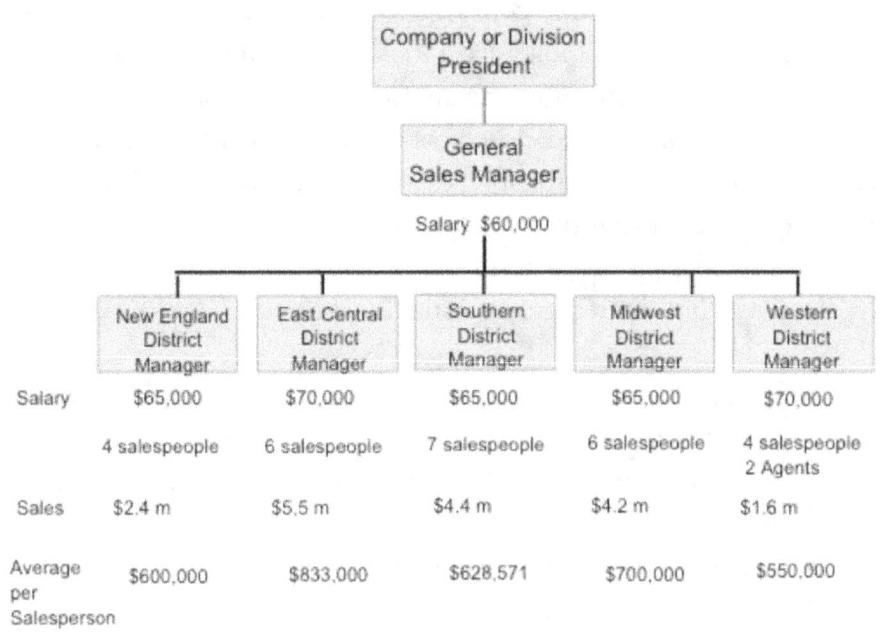

	New England District Manager	East Central District Manager	Southern District Manager	Midwest District Manager	Western District Manager
Salary	$65,000	$70,000	$65,000	$65,000	$70,000
	4 salespeople	6 salespeople	7 salespeople	6 salespeople	4 salespeople 2 Agents
Sales	$2.4 m	$5.5 m	$4.4 m	$4.2 m	$1.6 m
Average per Salesperson	$600,000	$833,000	$628,571	$700,000	$550,000

Savings:	Personnel	Salary		Expenses		
	2 Regional Managers	$170,000	+	$24,000	=	$194,000
	2 District Managers	$130,000	+	$36,000	=	$166,000
	2 Salespeople	$100,000	+	$35,000	=	$135,000
						$495,000

Less increased costs, raises & 2 agents
$100,000 + $20,000 = $120,000

Net savings $375,000

Total organizational savings: 4.1% of this $9.1 million sales company
35% of total department cost

Similarly, the general sales manager's span of control shows only five persons, which is below our stated ideal. In most companies, however, the sales manager would have other responsibilities, such as web sales, advertising, or market research, in addition to a heavy travel schedule.

All these changes, radical though they may seem, were made by following our simple rules concerning span of control and reporting relationships. We also took a hard look at the number of salespeople in all districts in relation to the amount of sales. Some districts will have to be studied more closely as the new organization structure settles in and expands to other departments. For the time being, however, an organizational analysis of the corporate hierarchy and the sales force is plenty to accomplish.

Here is what the reorganization has achieved:

- By eliminating two regional managers, we saved $194,000 in salaries and expenses.
- By eliminating two district managers, we saved another $166,000.
- By eliminating two salespeople, we saved $135,000.
- Total salaries and expenses eliminated: $495,000.

Another 40 percent (approximately $125,000) will be saved in fringes. Although fringes cannot be determined precisely by this macro analysis, neither should they be ignored or underestimated.

It will be necessary to put two new agents in the Western district at a cost of about $120,000 (a cost you pay only if they sell your products), and there will probably have to be raises amounting to about $20,000 to compensate for added responsibilities.

Thus the total saving will be about $495,000, minus the $120,000 for commissions and raises, for a net savings of $375,000, or 4.1 percent of the $9.1 million in sales. More significantly, this is a savings of 35 percent of total departmental costs ($375,000 savings divided by $1,055,000 total costs), and it does not include a probable reduction in fringes, which would result in an additional $150,000 in savings.

Remember also that with increasing energy costs and an expected return of inflation, any travel savings made now will translate into increasingly larger savings in the future. Recent economic trends have made it prohibitive for many companies to put salespeople out on the road, and tremendously burdensome for many others. The costs of automobiles, gasoline, insurance, meals, and lodging are not an insignificant part of your selling costs.

Note that even with the changes we have made, sales per salesperson still range between $550,000 and $833,666. Some companies will be able to average a much greater volume per salesperson, depending primarily on the profitability of the company, the product line, compound growth targets, and other particulars of the company in question. In other words, as with most of the examples throughout this text, we taken a suit off the rack; how you tailor the suit to your needs depends on your own circumstances.

First Weekend

At this stage you are one week into your program to maximize profits. During your first weekend, you have conducted both an organizational analysis and a ratio analysis of the entire company. The ratio analysis, as described in the previous chapter, has demonstrated what's possible over the long-term – a 300 percent increase in profits if you can replicate what each of the company's departments were doing correctly during the year they were operating at maximum efficiency. It has allowed you to return to work Monday morning armed with some very specific, targeted goals. And you are prepared to challenge your various department heads to meet these goals.

During this same first weekend, an organizational analysis, based on a company with $9.1 million in sales, has shown how to save 1.2 percent ($106,000) by reorganizing the manufacturing department, and 2.7 percent ($243,000) by reorganizing the sales department -- for a total of 3.9 percent, plus some travel expenses. And all this can be accomplished at home, during the first weekend after deciding to undertake a profit improvement plan.

First Week

During the *first week* you have begun to extend both the organizational and ratio analyses to other departments, such as sales. You have looked at your constant dollar chart and its supporting data to investigate the trend in sales per employee adjusted for inflation, and the variations and trends in your four employee categories of salaried exempt, salaried nonexempt, and direct and indirect labor. Also during the first week, you have compared your analyses with other comparable companies in your industry by using a financial reporting service, or simply by obtaining for free their annual reports and 10Ks from the SEC's EDGAR database.

First Month

During the first thirty days, this same reorganization and ratio analysis that you conducted for manufacturing and sales can also be applied elsewhere. Any area where you have supervisory personnel and pools of employees presents an opportunity to review, reduce costs, and improve efficiencies and control.

After a month, you should see your first results -- at least a 5 percent decrease in costs, which, as we saw in Chapter 1, can translate into a doubling or more of pretax profit.

The Rest of Your Life

Hopefully, the most important lesson you have learned during these first 30 days is that your operation, if it is at all typical, can stand a great deal of organizational tightening. Great progress can be made in one weekend, sitting in your most comfortable armchair, and then by implementing your plan during the next month. At the very least, you will gain a glimpse of the possibilities. These procedures should immediately become a permanent part of your operating procedures, and repeated at least once a year. No matter how efficient you believe your operation to be, a continuous, persistent program of organizational analysis and ratio analysis can lay the groundwork for the next steps in your overall effort to maximize profits, which will call for more in-depth measures that will require the better part of a year to complete.

Profit Improvement is Just Another Name for Cost Reduction

Before we move on to other strategies for maximizing profits, let's make clear that the concept of profit improvement can often be used interchangeably with the term "cost reduction." Ask yourself this: What is the ultimate goal of any comprehensive profit improvement program, whether you call it Six Sigma, lean manufacturing, quality improvement, or Gemba Kaizen?[18] It is to reduce your costs in relationship to output. If profit improvement is the glass of water half full, then cost reduction is the glass of water half empty.

There are many reasons why cost reduction is neglected as a strategy to improve profits. In the first place, it is often thought of as a dirty business. No executive wants to call an entire department into his or her office and tell employees that they have been performing inefficiently for the past five, ten, or twenty years. Secondly, there's nothing more uncomfortable than making significant layoffs, and cost reduction has absurdly become a euphemism for layoffs. Particularly at a manufacturing concern, where labor costs typically represent less than 10 percent of revenue, layoffs will not nearly be the most fertile area to explore.

Profit improvement by implementing cost efficiencies is not as flashy or dramatic as, say, a large increase in sales. But as we have already demonstrated, cost reduction is much more beneficial to a company's bottom line. A 30 percent increase in a company's sales might make the front page of a newspaper's business section; a comparable reduction in costs surely would not receive the same favorable treatment, even though it would be far less expensive and have a much more favorable impact on the company's bottom line.

---

18. In Japanese, "Gemba Kaizen" means "workplace productivity."

Another reason executives are reluctant to initiate a comprehensive profit improvement program is that very few of them know where to begin. Chief executives often are so busy with their day-to-day operations that they never find the time to implement vitally important cost reductions. The irony is that there is no more cost effective way for a top executive to spend their time. Regardless of the current position in the business cycle, cost reduction should be one of the first recourses of management when attempting to improve or stabilize profit. Chief executives should not wait until a stressful economic period to realize that reducing costs can immediately and effectively improve a company's bottom line performance. Delaying these profit improvement strategies can be suicidal.

CHAPTER THREE

Go Where the Money Is – Your Purchasing Department

Modern management theory has a lot to say about how to eliminate waste and improve efficiencies during the manufacturing process. A Six Sigma campaign, for example, will use a host of techniques to keep inventory costs down, eliminate shortages, and produce finished goods without waste. Lean manufacturing emphasizes the reduction of waste in all areas and in all forms, and 5S encompasses five Japanese terms aimed at creating a workplace suited for visually making certain that a foundation for a lean work place has been established.

Exhibit 3-1:
5S

Step	Japanese Name	English Translation	Description
S1	Seiri	Sort	Separate and remove unneeded items from needed ones
S2	Seiton	Simplify	Neatly arrange items for use
S3	Seiso	Scrub	Clean up the work area
S4	Seiketsu	Standardize	Sort, simplify, and scrub daily.
S5	Shitsuke	Sustain	Always follow the first four S's

Building Blocks

None of these modern techniques, however, take into account that maximizing profits needs to begin long before the materials reach the factory floor. It begins with the purchasing department, which in most manufacturing operations will control 40-50 percent of your sales dollar. This is the single most important message to be found anywhere in this text. Improvements in the way your purchasing department operates will have the greatest single positive impact on a manufacturing company's bottom line.

We cannot emphasize it enough: there is no more effective way to maximize profits than to focus on the cost, quality, and prompt delivery of materials and parts. That's where almost half of your company's revenue is going; that's where you can best maximize profits. What's more, improvements in this area can be accomplished with existing personnel, and without any significant expense or investment.

This is not to belittle the effectiveness of tools like 5S, Lean Manufacturing, and Six Sigma aimed at improving the manufacturing process. All these programs have been extremely successful at many, many companies. But at *all* companies, they should not be launched without an understanding of a few key common sense supply chain principles and techniques. This chapter will lay that foundation by establishing some basic purchasing rules and practices that form the building blocks that allow these other methods to be successful.

A Top Executive's Responsibility

We understand that in many organizations purchasing has morphed into a much broader logistical supply chain management system. But at its core, the goal of your purchasing department is a simple one: to purchase a specified material with the required quality and reliability, at the least expensive price, with the best terms, delivered on time, from a qualified supplier. This might seem like an obvious goal, but the importance of meeting it often goes unrecognized by top management.

As your company's top executive, you need to have your finger on the pulse of the department that spends almost half your revenue. There is no better way to have a positive impact on profitability. Particularly in today's economic climate, a small improvement in the way your company purchases materials can easily be the factor that turns red ink to black.

We've already shown in Chapter 1 that a 5 percent trimming of costs will translate into a more than 100 percent improvement in your bottom line. Now we are going to show you <u>how</u> to trim those costs.

You can start by making certain that you and all your top executives recognize and understand three key purchasing principles:

1. Don't be afraid of the purchasing department. As the company's top executive, make it your responsibility to understand the concepts in this chapter and the next, and be the driving force behind their implementation. Only your personal knowledge and attention will ensure that the purchasing department is all that it can be.

2. Purchase, don't expedite. Give your purchasing department a chance by avoiding single-sourced items, by standardizing as many parts as possible, and by allowing them the independence to be creative when negotiating with competing suppliers.

3. Concentrate efforts on "A" parts. In most manufacturing companies, 5-10 percent of parts and materials make up approximately 70-75 percent of total material costs. This concept, which we and others call ABC Inventory Control (some also call it ABC Stratification), will be explained in detail in the following chapter. But for now, it is important that each member of the purchasing department understands the importance of placing most of its focus on the selection and delivery of the company's most expensive "A" parts. Many of the specific purchasing techniques discussed in this chapter will not be nearly as effective without understanding and utilizing ABC Inventory Control or its equivalent as an overall operational premise.

ABC Inventory Control

Exhibit 3-2:
ABC Inventory Control

	% of Cost of Materials	% of Volume of Parts
"A" Parts	70 - 75	5 - 10
"B" Parts	20	20
"C" Parts	5 - 10	70 - 75

The single most important step toward establishing an effective, cost conscious purchasing department is the implementation of an ABC Inventory Control system under which all materials and parts purchased by a company are classified into three groups. An "A" classification signals that the item is in the most expensive category. These parts are critical to your company's operation. You will always want to know how many of these "A" items you have on hand. Too many will increase your inventory and overhead costs unnecessarily. Too few will bring your manufacturing operation to a standstill when they run out. Your buyers, analysts, and inventory control people -- everyone involved in purchasing -- should make it their business to know where the company stands with these items. "A" parts make up about 70-75 percent of the cost of all materials, but generally only 5-10 percent of the volume, or number, of parts. When properly controlled, this "A" group will lower costs and maximize profits. You may even want to further subdivide this category into "A" and "AA" parts, with even greater control being exercised over the "AA" parts.

A "B" part is not as expensive as an "A" part, but is more expensive than a "C" part. This is the middle group of parts that make up about 20 percent of the number of parts that are used, and approximately 20 percent of the dollars.

The "C" parts are the literal nuts and bolts of a company's operation - the bolts, the nuts, the screws, the washers -- the low-dollar, standard items that are frequently used. These items are inexpensive and can be bought in great volume once or twice a year. Because they represent 70-75 percent of the volume but only 5-10 percent of inventory investment, they can be heavily stocked with a minimum of control.

By dividing all materials into these three categories, emphasis can be placed on the "A" parts. That is where your company is making its largest investment, so these are the items that require the most attention, even though they make up only a small percentage of the total number of parts.

Do the math yourself. If materials represent 45 percent of your sales dollar, and "A" parts make up 70 percent of the total cost of materials, then this small handful of parts represent almost a third (45% x 70% = 31.5%) of your company's costs. It stands to reason, therefore, that the purchasing techniques discussed in the balance of this chapter will be most effective with these "A" parts.

For "A" and "AA" parts, the purchasing department should be using blanket, or long-term contracts in which the supplier promises to re-supply your company as needed at an agreed-upon price over the length of the contract. Your purchasing department staff should also maintain close contact with suppliers and potential suppliers in order to be certain of their ability to meet the company's production requirements for these important "A" parts. The purchasing department needs to know, for example, if a supplier is having any difficulty that could jeopardize either the schedule or the quality of the delivery.

The purpose of ABC Inventory Control is to place your resources and your profit improvement expertise on these most important items. By keeping careful track of "A" parts, an efficient inventory turn can be created. Large amounts of cash will not be tied up in expensive parts waiting idly to be placed into a finished product, and your production process will not suddenly and unexpectedly be caught short without an expensive, hard-to-find "A" item.

Don't Be Afraid of the Purchasing Department

Like many top executives, you may not have firsthand knowledge of the purchasing function. Executives tend to supervise most closely the area (or areas) with which they are most familiar. You most likely have come up through sales, marketing, manufacturing, engineering, or finance, and you may be reluctant to become closely involved with purchasing due to a lack of understanding of the department. This is a serious mistake. The company president needs to have intimate knowledge about how the company is spending almost half its sales dollar.

Don't allow your unfamiliarity with purchasing tempt you to leave the responsibility of proper purchasing techniques to a subordinate. You will have a chief of purchasing, of course. But it is your job to understand the importance of treating the purchasing department as the top priority of any effort to maximize profits. Take the time to learn the various opportunities discussed in this and the next chapter. Make certain your top management also spends time learning about the purchasing function. In fact, rotate each one of them into the purchasing department, giving them specific tasks that will force them to utilize the principles discussed within these two chapters. By the same token, purchasing personnel should receive training and practical experience in accounting, manufacturing, and engineering in order to broaden their knowledge and awareness. Rotate them from assignment to assignment and, whenever possible, between such disciplines as industrial engineering, inventory and production control, and accounting. That will ensure buyers do not become stale, and that they have the broad experience necessary to understand the impact of their decisions and the various profit improvement techniques described in these pages. Most important, they will feel like a valuable and integral part of the company. Rotation will also eliminate the likelihood of an individual buying from certain suppliers over a long period of time and thereby establishing a personal, rather than a business, relationship with that supplier.

As an aside, rotation of responsibilities should not be limited to the purchasing area. It should be instituted among all capable newcomers in a company. This will allow them a better overall knowledge of the organization, which is so invaluable once they reach the executive level, and will enable them to identify the areas they enjoy the most and in which they are most capable.

Not only should you take responsibility for understanding proper purchasing techniques yourself, also make certain there is direct access between you and the head of purchasing. The purchasing chief, who should be considered a top department head, should have the ear and confidence of top management. After all, that individual most likely controls the largest share of the company's money.

We recommend that the purchasing director report directly to the company president or chief operating officer. This runs contrary to a concept that has been gaining in popularity -- the institution of a materials manager. While there are exceptions, in the vast majority of cases this type of position is not a good idea in small and midsize companies. First of all, it downgrades purchasing to one or two levels below the company head, so that the steward of your main cost segment is now reporting to a materials manager, who frequently reports to the head of manufacturing. Demoting the purchasing department two levels puts a lower salary level on the job and makes it subject to pressures from people who are frequently interested in output regardless of outcome. The head of purchasing then becomes an expeditor, rather than a creative contributor toward maximizing profits.

Secondly, creating a one-over-two supervisory position (instead of our sought-after one-over-seven to one-over-ten recommended in Chapter 2) defies good organizational practice. In addition, a materials manager who has come up through production control generally will not have the necessary background to supervise purchasing intelligently. Having procurement and production control within the same department, especially as a company grows and becomes more complex, would be like putting manufacturing and sales under one department head. By having the purchasing department report directly to the company president, any change in material costs, deliveries, market trends, or possible component substitution can be evaluated quickly so that the best possible business decision can be made.

As part of your supervision, ask your purchasing head for at least a monthly report which summarizes weekly or monthly activities and emphasizes recent price increases and cost savings (as well as cost avoidance) successes. If a 5 percent reduction in material costs has been established as the company's objective, this report should analyze how well that goal is being met. Especially in periods of inflation or commodity price fluctuations, a weekly cost index of key (or "A") parts is essential to developing your own intelligent and timely pricing moves that will help protect profit margins.

Meet with your purchasing head regularly to review these reports. Ask the purchasing staff to explain why they have chosen a particular supplier. If your purchasing department is sourcing a particular part or material from a supplier because "that's the way we've always done it" or because "it's worked well in the past," these aren't good enough reasons. You can immediately assume that there is something fundamentally wrong with the way the department is operating. Another red flag is if the same suppliers are sourced year after year. Ask specifically if for every purchased item, a second and third source was rejected in favor of the current supplier. Some purchasing agents tend to protect their chosen suppliers for long periods of time.

Above all, don't isolate yourself from the purchasing department or your head of purchasing. Meet with them regularly. Become involved.

Purchase, Don't Expedite

As company president, be certain of the caliber and integrity of the purchasing staff, and make them feel a part of the management team working to keep costs down and profits up. All too often, purchasing is treated as a perfunctory, clerical, or expediting function.

Allow your purchasing department to use its creativity, imagination, and professional experience to purchase the highest quality parts and material at the lowest possible prices, with the best terms. Do not treat the department as if it were ordering out for coffee. Do not put them into an expediting mode by poor forecasting or by a lack of proper sales and manufacturing planning.

The purchasing department can and should provide direct, important input to the company president from the front lines when it comes to such decisions as make-or-buy, redesign, supplier selection, alternate sourcing, availability, and pricing. This department can also be of great help in keeping investment down, inventories balanced, and run-outs minimized.

In analyzing a purchasing department's effectiveness, ask yourself one simple question: Is it a clerical operation or a professional one? Does the purchasing manager have the necessary authority to make management decisions? Anyone, if told to do so, can send out a purchase order to a given supplier for a specific part. But a purchasing manager should be able to do much more than that by taking into account the many variables that enter into most any purchasing agreement. The purchasing manager should, for example, be able to suggest to management that a savings could be made by changing suppliers, by manufacturing the part in-house, by buying in volume at a discount, or by taking delivery in monthly quantities.

If people are treated like clerks, they will become clerks. If they are treated like professionals, they have the opportunity to become professionals. When the purchasing staff knows they are valued for the special skills they possess and are encouraged to think like managers, they become an immensely valuable asset to the company.

Along these same lines, a purchasing department must be given the freedom and time to use its cost cutting skills. If the sales or manufacturing department demands a volume of parts for immediate delivery, the hands of the purchasing chief are tied. Not only will the purchasing department be unable to negotiate the best price, but every aspect of making that part available will be unnecessarily costly.

Transportation and packaging costs will be at a premium, and there certainly won't be time to sit down with the sales, manufacturing, and engineering departments to make any kind of redesign or needs costs analysis. Proper sourcing, negotiated contracts, and suggested improvements also won't be possible.

A purchasing department should not, in other words, simply be instructed to order a given number of parts. Rather, it should be told that a specific number of these parts will be needed over a particular period of time, and be asked to come up with recommendations on how best to obtain them. The buyers now can negotiate with outside suppliers by conducting a proper sourcing job based on the item's required quality, volume, and delivery; previous prices; possible lower-priced substitutes; and the best manufacturing and vending methods. Hardly just ordering out for coffee.

Since the purchasing staff are trained to interface with the outside world, relations with suppliers should, for the most part, be limited to that department. Engineering or manufacturing personnel should not represent the company to outside suppliers except when their expertise is required, and even then only in concert with the appropriate member of your purchasing staff.

It is the purchasing department's job to purchase, no one else's. Do not allow, for example, your engineering department to request a particular supplier's product without the "or equal" phrase, or to specify a "special" without collaborating with the purchasing department to determine if an off-the-shelf standard item will suffice. Such actions tend to foster the famous NIH (Not Invented Here) syndrome, whereby your company's engineers are unable to look objectively at parts or products that they themselves have designed. (See Chapter 5 for a more detailed discussion of redesigning parts.)

Competition Is Key

Competition is the key to any free enterprise system, and this axiom is particularly true in the purchasing area. But creating an environment in which competition thrives among suppliers means much more than simply encouraging bidding wars. Equally important is to make sure suppliers and purchasers alike can be creatively challenged to work together to improve the products being purchased.

The centerpiece to creating an environment in which competition thrives is to make an open door policy your first golden rule of purchasing. Too many companies limit visits from salespeople to particular days or hours. Salespeople should know that the door to the purchasing department is always open to them, and that a purchasing agent will not refuse to see them during working hours. In fact, display your open door policy prominently in your lobby as a reminder to both your own employees and to suppliers who pay your company a visit that competition is encouraged

In today's global economy you may be just as likely to receive a lower price, a higher quality product, or better terms from the website of a company in Europe or Asia than you are from a salesperson who is able to knock on your door. Prominently display the policy on your own website and as a URL link that is a routine part of your response to salespeople who approach your company seeking business.

Exhibit 3-3: Open Door Policy

Dear Supplier:

At a time when it is becoming an increasingly common practice to restrict the days and hours that salespeople may call, we at PIWB Inc. want you to know that you are welcome at any time or on any day that we conduct business. This is our policy.

We look to you for ideas, suggestions, and creative solutions that will enable us to reduce our costs and to offer the highest standards of quality and service to our customers. We don't think these priorities can or should be limited to particular days or hours.

We want you to know that our suppliers are always welcome. We appreciate your interest in our needs and we value your assistance and advice. Since quite a few of us in management came up through selling, we recognize that the salesperson's job is not an easy one. We don't intend to make it any harder than it is by establishing arbitrary restrictions.

We need you and we ask for your help. We know you won't fail us, and if we fail to treat you fairly, please let me know personally. Thank you for coming in.

Sincerely yours,
Mathew Figgie
Chairman

An open door policy needs to be more than just rhetoric. Purchasing departments often fall into bad habits – for example, they may remain with one particular supplier because they have been doing business together for years. Just because a particular salesperson or supplier has historically been reliable, or even managed to furnish a product for the company during a critical shortage period, does not mean that supplier has necessarily remained competitive. Undue allegiance to one supplier will discourage newcomers from approaching your purchasing department with competitive bids, and reflects negatively on the department's integrity. When procurement is not fairly or honestly conducted, the word passes quickly among suppliers.

By making suppliers feel welcome, you will generate competition among them to your own benefit, often enabling your purchasing department to negotiate better terms from your original suppliers. But that does not mean when a purchasing agent receives a lower set of prices or better terms or quality from a new supplier, your company should automatically turn around and ask the present supplier to match the new terms. Instead, the fact that the new salesperson has discounted the price or offered better service at your invitation should earn that supplier at least some of the business, providing he or she represents a qualified supplier. Otherwise, your purchasing department will earn a deserved reputation as a place that does not reward aggressiveness or creativity, and soon enough new suppliers will no longer bother to try to get your business.

One effective way to stimulate competition is to display publicly a product board listing certain products that the company regularly purchases, or new products that will be needed in the future. That way, salespeople can see instantly where they stand on products they are trying to sell, and on products they may not have thought your company needs. Products on the board should be rotated periodically. Again, this list can be maintained on a chalk board for all to see, but should also be posted prominently on your company's website. In this economy plenty of new suppliers, often from all over the world, should be seeking your business. If they know what you are looking for, they will be able to offer not only better terms, but also design change or material substitution recommendations.

Avoid Single-Sourced Items

The purchasing department plays a critical role as the first line of offense in maximizing profits, and should avoid locking itself into one supplier. Again, competition is the name of the game. If for any reason one supplier submits what you consider to be an unreasonable price increase, you should, if at all possible, have an alternative supplier on standby. This way, your company will never find itself in a sudden bind if a primary supplier experiences a strike, goes out of business, discontinues a particular item, or suffers a fire or other natural disaster.

Every effort should be made to obtain competitive quotations from various suppliers at least once a year; more often on your most expensive "A" parts, particularly if cost increases do not appear justified. With commodity price fluctuations and the frequent and often dramatic price increases that can occur quickly these days for certain natural resources, buyers should be able to determine what factors have increased the cost of an item. It might be the cost of labor, overhead, raw materials, packaging, transportation, or outside services. By isolating various component costs, you will be able to reconstruct the item's overall pricing structure. And remember, your "A" items should command special attention.

While competition among suppliers is crucial, there are also advantages to sourcing a number of products with a single supplier. It saves administrative costs, is more practical in terms of developing a rapport with the supplier, and allows the purchaser more room for negotiation.

Standardize Materials

Whenever possible, the use of exotic or unusual materials should be avoided, since they will almost always cost a premium and tie your hands when negotiating for better terms. Standard, common materials are less expensive, and often a single part can be substituted for a wide range of items without sacrificing efficiency, durability, or quality.

Suppliers, too, recognize that limiting the choices they offer is to their advantage. It used to be, for example, that steel manufacturers offered a wide range of materials in terms of alloy content, size, thickness, and other specifications. In today's environment, however, if it's even possible to find an exotic, low-demand item, you will either pay dearly for it, or be required to place a very large minimum order, or both. To be most effective, standardization should be instituted at the very outset of a product's design, which is why it is so important that the purchasing and engineering departments are familiar with each other and routinely work together.

As part of the effort to standardize materials, avoid engineering-sourced items. When the specifications given to a purchasing department are tied to an engineer's blueprints, there is little opportunity to negotiate for the best price or terms. If the design specifications for a concrete mixer, for example, call for a special, instead of a standard, off-the-shelf cylinder, the purchasing department has no choice but to ask for bids for exactly such a cylinder, even if that means paying a higher price or accommodating a longer lead time. This kind of engineering-sourced item severely limits the negotiating position a purchaser ordinarily has with suppliers, and thus limits the ways in which the purchasing department can help maximize profits.

Even after the fact, a creative member of your purchasing staff can take a set of blueprints, and work with your engineers to take advantage of the standardization that has taken place in virtually every industry. This is why it is so important for your purchaser to have at least a basic understanding of other parts of the company, particularly engineering and sales. In many cases, for example, a buyer can take an existing set of blueprints and find a standard grade of bolt or cap screw that can be used throughout the entire application. This reduces the number of different parts to be used and increases the volume of the item to be purchased, thereby saving money. Unfortunately, this is an area in which engineers seem to prefer "specials" rather than the more common, standardized nuts, screws, bolts, and other "C" or low cost parts.

Sometimes standardization can actually mean paying more for certain parts if the overall result is to maximize profits. This may seem counterintuitive, but consider a common situation whereby blueprint specifications call for components of an assembly to be of various material types, thus resulting in buying small quantities of many different materials. It might be more cost effective to standardize on the strongest material, paying more for material per pound but reducing overall costs due to volume reduction. Multiple orders, for example, even if less expensive per unit, will force the purchasing department to complete individual purchase orders, segregate the material, identify it, and handle it separately. All these bookkeeping and time consuming tasks are costly, and increase the dangers of excess scrap and obsolescence. Remember, we are concerned with maximizing the bottom line, which may mean slight cost increases in some areas in order to save greater sums overall.

Cooperation Between Departments

Due to the fact that purchasing agents have contacts with the outside supplier world, by the very nature of the job they have access to what is happening in the marketplace. They are, therefore, in many ways in the best position to provide information to the rest of the company as to future fluctuations in the price and availability of the raw materials instrumental to the company's operations.

Your company's other departments, including engineering, manufacturing, and sales, must make their own priorities perfectly clear to the procurement staff. While price, quality, and service will always be important, there will be some instances when a purchasing department will be asked to emphasize one priority over the other.

A much better strategy is to get your purchasing staff involved early in the strategic planning process. While it is rare that an important, long-term decision is made unilaterally by the purchasing department, there are at least five management functions in which the purchasing department should play an important role. They are:

1. Product redesign (Chapter 5).
2. Value analysis (Chapter 5).
3. Make-or-buy decisions (Chapter 5).
4. Pricing (Chapter 7).
5. Sales forecasting (Chapter 6).

Uncertain Economic Climate

When a company is in need of a particular part, standard operating procedure is for the purchasing department to request bids from at least three or four different suppliers. These suppliers are sent drawings and other documents related to the desired part, spelling out everything from design specifications, quantities required, type of material to be used, and the needed delivery date. The purchasing department then receives a quote from each supplier.

When the economic situation is relatively stable, there often is not a tremendous difference between the high and low price of any particular item. A low price might be 20¢ a pound, while the premium rate might be 22¢ or 23¢. But those days seem to be over for good. Even with low inflation rates in recent years, which may or may not be sustained given our huge federal deficits, fluctuating commodity prices and the uncertain cost of credit can still cause prices to fluctuate, sometimes dramatically. In fact, in an uncertain economic climate, price and availability can change from one month to the next. Factors beyond your control can either create sudden shortages, or drive up the price of some materials well in excess of the consumer or producer price indices. All this makes proper purchasing techniques more vital than ever for a company's successful operation.

More Than Just Price

Price is often the single most important reason to choose one supplier over another, but it is by no means the only factor. Quality and reliability can be equally important. Other variables to consider include credit terms, distance from the supplier to your plant, the cost and reliability of delivery, and a supplier's creative contributions. Be sure to make your company accessible to new and innovative ideas. In today's world, fresh techniques and innovations are being created every day from the unlikeliest of places.

Price is important, of course, but sometimes you should be wary of a supplier, particularly if inexperienced, who is offering a lower price than everyone else. One lesson we've learned along the way is that any price can be beaten, and we have seen the consequences when suppliers emphasize low price over everything else: they go out of business and leave their customers in a bind. The head of the industry association for screw machine product companies once told us that for a decade or more, 10-15 of its members went out of business or were sold each and every year, even while the number of total machines in the United States remained constant. This meant that when one company failed, another group bought the machinery and gave it a try. Clearly, this 10-15 percent of the companies did not have an adequate understanding of their costs, but they offered great prices for the short periods of time they remained in business. We will have a lot more to say about proper pricing techniques in Chapter 7.

A good purchasing agent considers an almost limitless number of factors besides price before signing a contract with a supplier. The lowest-priced supplier, for example, might be located in a distant city or country and therefore have higher transportation costs or an unacceptable delivery date. Another supplier may be offering a particularly low price, but only for a minimum run of 300 pieces. This doesn't do you much good if you only need 200. In yet another case, you might happen to know of a supplier who, just after giving you a quote, lost a large order. This supplier may be willing to lower its bid now that its factories need the work. Or maybe the best price can be obtained by agreeing to have your own truck pick up the pieces from a supplier who had a low bid but high delivery costs.

Today, with the price of fuel fluctuating wildly from one month to the next, lowering transportation costs can be another extremely important component of proper purchasing techniques. One tipoff that a purchasing department is not doing its job properly is when a purchase order does not specify routing instructions. If the buyer's instructions to a supplier are to ship the applicable item "best way," or if there are no instructions at all, that item, more often than not, is not going to be transported by the least expensive or quickest means. It is the buyer's job, not the supplier's, to make certain that all costs, from production through delivery, are as low as possible, and that the items are delivered on schedule at the correct specifications, and without damage.

Packaging is another area in which profit improvement measures can be implemented. A glance at a carton of ball bearings, for example, might tell a purchaser that the packaging is unnecessarily complex. It is triple-wall corrugated when it could just as effectively be single-wall corrugated, or it is being packaged in a crate instead of an inexpensive container.

Your purchasing department should also routinely consider vendor stocking. Let suppliers pay to inventory the material; it is frequently to their advantage anyway, because they can get longer, more efficient run lengths. With some type of guaranteed use over a blanket period, the supplier is protected. Both partners win. From your company's point of view, items shipped periodically mean faster turnover and less inventory investment. This becomes even more of a key factor when interest costs are high or credit difficult to obtain.

All these variables have to be weighed by a purchasing agent who can juggle the entire range of possible solutions before coming up with the best price and delivery terms, balanced against the best-suited product and most reliable supplier.

Work Creatively With Suppliers

A company should do its utmost to keep abreast of those suppliers who can save it money. The only way a company is going to be aware of the different possibilities for maximizing profit is to view suppliers as experts in their particular fields. Buyers should analyze what suppliers have to offer, then make a decision as to whether it is appropriate for the company's needs.

Recent shortages of raw materials have made it even more vital for purchasing departments to keep track of trends and maintain a close, trusting relationship with suppliers. Copper, bauxite, tungsten, and chromium, as well as virtually all petroleum products, are a few items that will have to be followed closely. Particularly with these materials, difficult economic times have caused many small suppliers to go out of business, leaving relatively few sources for certain vital materials. This means companies frequently have to negotiate with fewer suppliers, increasing the importance of creating and maintaining a close relationship between buyer and seller. Develop a rapport with suppliers so that they are aware of your demands and so that they, because of *your* reliability, will continue to service your account even when shortages do occur. At the same time, don't surrender price consciousness. Once a buyer has decided to do business with a particular supplier, and when a general, ballpark price has been agreed upon, the purchasing department should not necessarily accept the quoted price. The philosophy of everyone from the company president down to the most junior buyer should be that costs can *always* be reduced.

If, for example, a purchasing department accepts multiple quotes on an item and one supplier comes in at $10 and everyone else comes in at $11, the assumption still must be that there is fat even in the

$10 figure. The purchasing staff should sit down with the $10 supplier with the understanding that they want to do business with them, but that they also want to find ways the $10 figure can be reduced. This is the time when a buyer's experience and expertise come into play.

Most companies are not in a position to foresee every trend in usage, consumption, and availability that might affect them. In fact, because of the volatile state of the economy, and because such a large percentage of many raw materials must be imported, shortages are bound to occur and prices are apt to fluctuate, sometimes dramatically and sometimes in a very short period of time. This, combined with the cost and scarcity of credit, puts pressure on suppliers to keep inventories low. At the same time, business recovery spurts can create sudden shortages and long lead times. As a result, many suppliers, particularly small ones, are unable to maintain the inventories necessary to meet the immediate demands of all companies. This just adds to the importance of working closely with your suppliers, and having a backup plan in place if your primary supplier runs into a problem.

Although not the focus of this book, supply chain management has evolved considerably over the last twenty years. Today's purchasing manager can consult a variety of internet sites, like globalspec.com and alibaba.com, for access to potential suppliers on a worldwide basis. Additionally, electronic bidding or e-bids are becoming a more popular way to engage competition and lower component costs. E-bidding used to be confined to the automotive industry, but that is no longer the case.

Ethical Behavior

Because the bulk of the sales dollar revolves around the purchasing department, and because the best way to reduce material costs is to allow buyers the freedom to negotiate, purchasing is also, unfortunately, an area that can create a temptation to commit unethical acts. Make certain that every member of your purchasing department is beyond reproach. Make it perfectly clear to all concerned that gifts and gratuities have no place in the ethical business transactions between buyer and seller. This theme should be strongly emphasized by all people involved in corporate procurement. In fact, it is a good idea for the director of purchasing to send out a letter at the beginning of each year to every supplier reaffirming this policy.

Certain purchasing areas are particularly susceptible to unethical behavior. For example, a key responsibility of the purchasing department, in addition to procurement, is to sell scrap, obsolete, or excess material. In order to maximize the return to the corporation, this needs to be done in an objective and comprehensive manner. If it requires knowledge the purchasing department does not have, the purchasing manager should get the necessary help and expertise.

End of the Month Syndrome

Companies need to be diligent about avoiding another pitfall, which we call the "End-of-the-Month Syndrome." The way this syndrome is allowed to occur, and its painful repercussions, could easily fill an entire chapter by itself, mainly because every department can fall prey to it.

Take, for example, the case of a company with a monthly goal of shipping $10 million worth of its product in order to reach a yearly sales target of $120 million. Ideally, shipments should be spaced throughout the month so that all employees have a steady work load each and every day. Typically, however, the first week of the month is inordinately slow. Everyone is just recovering from the hectic last week of the previous month. People are happy to take it easy for a few days or to catch up on paper work. If a part does not arrive on time, or it arrives but is defective, or if a customer changes his order at the last minute, the delay is taken in stride, as long as it occurs during the first half of the month. "Plenty of time to correct the problem," is the general feeling, even if the entire manufacturing process has to be delayed until the part is available.

Before you know it, however, it is the middle of the month, and only $1 million worth of goods has been shipped. Suddenly the manufacturing plant is in chaos, with everyone scurrying around in a mad dash to ship $9 million worth of goods in the last ten working days of the month. This inevitably results in poor productivity and wasteful expenditures.

In such a scenario, the purchasing department is placed in a particularly untenable situation. As the end of the month approaches, pressures mount to obtain needed supplies, regardless of cost, so that the company's monthly quota can be met. This is a sure way to lose control of costs. Quality control will also suffer, as there will be undue pressure to ship everything that comes off the manufacturing floor, ignoring a minor defect that might otherwise have caused it to be rejected. There is also a tendency to reach into the next month and pull out all the "cherries" (the good stuff), a decision which will only exacerbate the problem the following month.

Too many manufacturing operations operate in this kind of constant atmosphere of crisis. Every department must be aware of the dangers of the End of the Month Syndrome and plan in advance to avoid it. The marketing department, for example, should not allow customers to frivolously change orders at the last minute, and each department should schedule its tasks so that it is prepared to deliver a consistent performance throughout the month.

Summary

Always remember it is unlikely any area within your company has more to offer in the effort to maximize profits than the purchasing department. And no area is more often overlooked. Continually keep in mind these key purchasing principles:

- The effort to maximize profits begins well before the actual manufacturing process gets underway.
- Be certain that you understand the principles laid out in this chapter well enough so that you are able to properly direct and regularly evaluate your head of purchasing, and coordinate purchasing efforts with engineering, manufacturing, and sales.
- Concentrate most of your efforts on the 5-10 percent of your parts that make up 70-75 percent of your material costs.

- Individual buyers must use their experience, common sense, and imagination to work with their suppliers to continually come up with ways in which the purchasing function can contribute to the company's overall goal of maximizing profits.
- The ever-changing economic situation, the finite quantities of certain raw materials, and the unending supply of new parts, products, and technologies make it vital for purchasing personnel to be highly qualified, alert, and have direct communication with the company president and those in charge of key departments, particularly engineering and manufacturing.
- Encourage competition among suppliers, comparing more factors than just price.
- Avoid single-sourced items.
- Standardize materials whenever possible.

The next chapter continues to concentrate on how material costs can be cut. But first we will end this chapter with a number of brief case studies that illustrate many of the themes discussed in the previous pages.

Exhibit 3-4:
Negotiation Case Study -- Work With Your Suppliers

One supplier can guarantee an early delivery date, but is $20 higher per item than the lowest bid received. A phone call indicates that this supplier's costs are high because of being forced, for whatever reason, to pay an exorbitant rate for the relatively small amounts of steel required for the particular item. The buyer may be in a position to provide the steel from the company's own inventory, or perhaps the buyer simply knows where it can be purchased inexpensively. Or discussions with the company's engineering and factory people may identify a more standardized steel that is readily available at a much lower cost. The buyer, by *telling the supplier to quote the job excluding the steel, will in this way find the path to the lowest price.*

Exhibit 3-5:
Negotiation Case Study -- Every Price Can Be Beat

The purchasing department and a supplier sit down to discuss ways in which costs can be cut on a $10 item. First it is determined that shipping the item ten to a carton instead of six will immediately reduce the cost by 20¢. Through further investigation, the buyer learns that the aluminum required had been ordered to outdated specifications and that the current standard for this item is a better quality, less expensive grade aluminum. This reduces the cost per item by another 40¢. Then the purchasing department asks the supplier why transportation costs were estimated at $1, and the answer is unsatisfactory. The purchasing department can arrange for a company-owned truck to pick up and deliver the goods.

Now the purchasing department can buy the same item at $8.40 per unit ($10 - (20¢ + 40¢ + $1)). At least most of this $1.60 savings will go right to the company, since the cost of the company-owned truck will be nowhere near as expensive as $1 per unit. The truck may even be returning from another job empty, in which case there will be virtually no additional cost. Or perhaps the supplier will agree to meet the new $8.40 price, including delivery.

Exhibit 3-6:
Negotiation Case Study -- Vendor Stocking

Your company uses 4,000 pieces of a particular item annually. In the past, you have always ordered 1,000 pieces four times *per year. At your urging, however, your purchasing department sits down with the supplier and learns that every three months you are being charged $5 for each piece, plus setup costs of $1,000, which include the tooling and fixturing that have to be brought into the line only for as long as it takes to fill the order. The setup costs are $1,000 whether the order is for 1,000 pieces or 4,000 pieces. The supplier agrees to run the full year's requirements and store them, shipping to the company in periodic partial quantities. The purchasing department then negotiates to keep most of the $3,000 savings for the company, rather than allow it to go to the supplier.*

Exhibit 3-7:
Negotiation Case Study -- Early Commitment

A supplier's peak season is January through March. From April to June it tends to lay people off. Your purchasing department agrees to give this supplier an order in May, with the understanding that the supplier will have to warehouse the material until it is needed. By committing early to an order with a cyclical supplier, a purchasing department can often reduce the supplier's costs, a savings that can be passed on to your company.

Exhibit 3-8:
Negotiation Case Study -- Packaging Costs

A manufacturer of golf balls packages them in three-sleeve containers, and then four sleeves to a box with a filler. The box, in other words, is too large for the four sleeves so a filler is needed to occupy the excess space. Your new purchasing agent, after making certain marketing agrees that a smaller package will not detract from the salability of the product, shrinks the box, eliminating the need for a filler. Costs are reduced by eliminating unnecessary material, as well as by making the total product smaller and lighter, and therefore less expensive to transport.

Exhibit 3-9:
Negotiation Case Study -- Lead Time From Europe

A company uses 10,000 forgings annually. Its European supplier has always had two requirements: that the company purchase full container loads of the product, and that the lead time be between 6 and 9 months. After a face-to-face meeting in Europe to review the supplier's manufacturing process, the purchaser is able to reduce the minimum order to demand quantity only, with a lead time of less than three months. This effectively reduces the company's average raw inventory by more than 30 percent, releasing about $300,000 in cash.

Exhibit 3-10:
Negotiation Case Study -- Beware of Unreliable, Faraway Suppliers

A company wanting to broaden its supply base into low-cost countries contracts with a Chinese supplier to sew and deliver fleece sweatshirts. After sending the raw material to the supplier in China, the purchasing agent is having difficulty securing a ship date. The agent is finally told by the supplier that it has received a better offer from another U.S. company, but that the fleece cannot be returned because it has been used to practice sewing the sweatshirts, and any remaining fleece has been scrapped. The purchasing agent has little practical recourse except to absorb the loss. Purchasing departments need to be keenly aware of each supplier's reputation, process capability, quality, and integrity.

CHAPTER FOUR

KEEP ASKING, WHERE ARE YOU SPENDING YOUR DOLLARS?

In the previous chapter, the classification of parts through an ABC inventory control system was briefly outlined as part of an overall, comprehensive strategy to reduce costs in the purchasing area. ABC classification is perhaps the single most important technique a purchasing department can use to place itself in a position to maximize profits.

This chapter will offer a more in-depth discussion of the ABC system, a statistical method of dividing up inventory. Quite simply, experience has taught us that in the typical universe of parts:

- 5-10 percent of parts will represent 70-75 percent of material costs, but only 5-10 percent of shortages. These are your "A" parts.
- 20 percent of parts will represent 20 percent of material costs, and 20 percent of shortages. These are your "B" parts.
- 70-75 percent of parts will represent 5-10 percent of material costs and 70-75 percent of shortages. These are your "C" parts.

This means that in order to maximize profits, reduce obsolescence, and turn your inventory faster, you want to source, negotiate, control, cost redesign, and otherwise concentrate your efforts on the 5-30 percent of your parts ("A"s and "B"s). The other 70-75 percent can be bought in large quantities with a minimum of inventory controls, since both the investment and obsolescence will be relatively small. Such a program should materially reduce shortages, as will be explained shortly.

Many company presidents, when told of the importance of classifying component parts, will argue that theirs is a 40,000-part company and it is impossible to keep track of 40,000 individual parts. (For some reason we can never understand, 40,000 seems to be the magic number.) But in a 40,000-part company, only 4,000 will be "A" parts that require the most attention. Only 8,000 will be "B" parts needing moderate attention. The remaining 28,000 parts will be "C"s requiring no posting records at all. Hence, a 40,000-part system really becomes a 10,000-12,000-part system, which is easily handled by your computerized system.

At one company we managed, we once reduced a truck to its basic parts. The results shown in Exhibit 4-1 may surprise you, but they represent a typical ABC distribution.

Understanding the Basics

Like every other strategy discussed in this book, the first step is for the company's top executive to understand the why and the how. Why and how will an ABC system help to maximize profits? Because by focusing on where your company's dollars reside and are expended, your efforts will have the maximum impact. Now you just have to know how to get started. Many presidents and chief executive officers of small to midsize companies are unfamiliar with the ABC system, and therefore do not know where to begin, even if they are convinced of the system's tremendous value.

The simplest, most effective initial step for a president or chief executive officer who is unfamiliar with the ABC system is to understand the 80-20 rule, and then, once adapted to their particular company, immediately take advantage of it. Remember, in the typical manufacturing company, 20 percent of finished items will provide 80 percent of sales. As the company's head of operations, you should begin by learning the identity of this 20 percent of your company's products. In turn, within this 20 percent, make sure you know which components make up 80 percent of their cost. This small handful of parts are the ones that should receive attention first and foremost,

EXHIBIT 4-1 ABC Profile

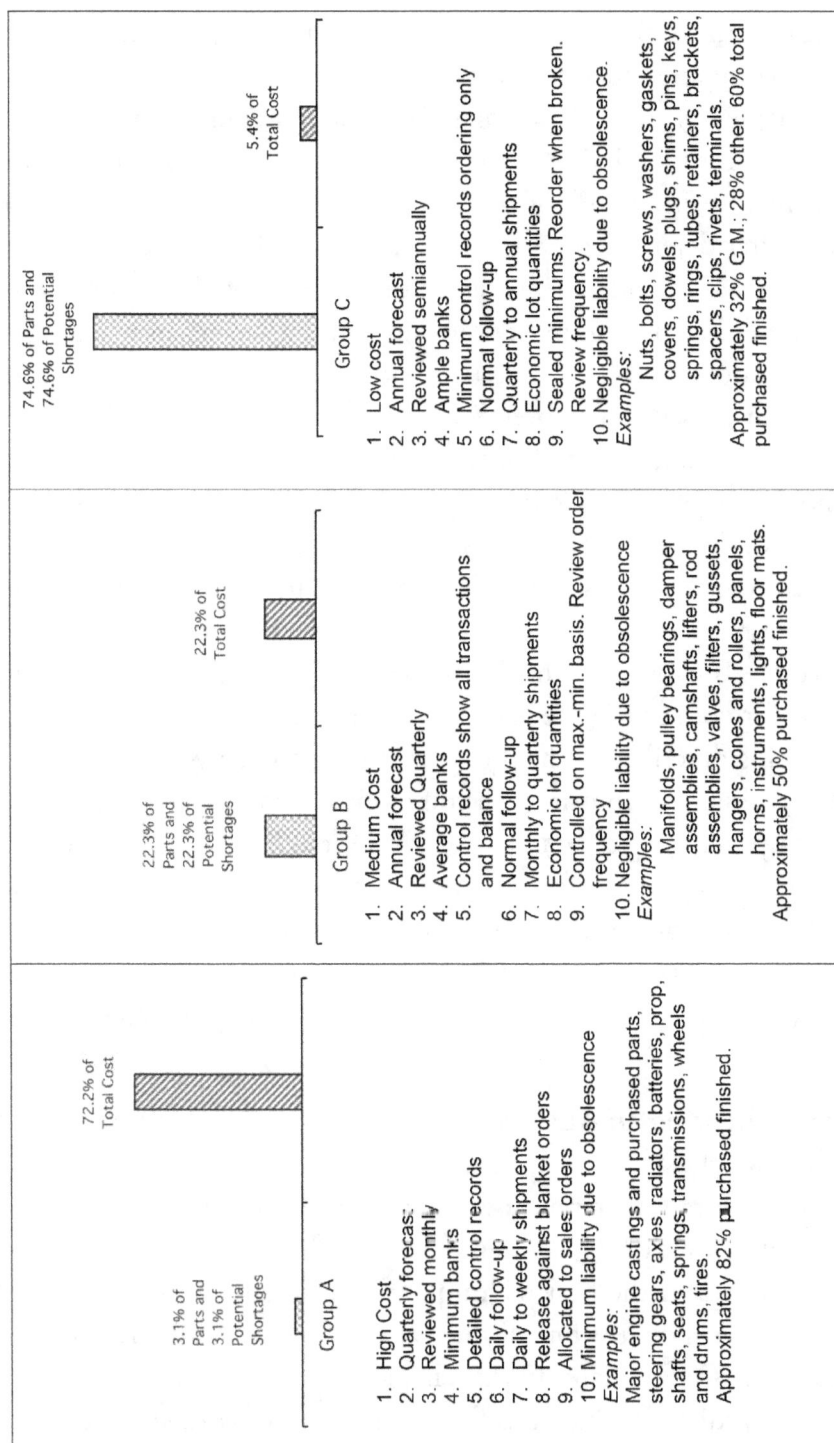

3.1% of Parts and 3.1% of Potential Shortages

72.2% of Total Cost

Group A

1. High Cost
2. Quarterly forecast
3. Reviewed monthly
4. Minimum banks
5. Detailed control records
6. Daily follow-up
7. Daily to weekly shipments
8. Release against blanket orders
9. Allocated to sales orders
10. Minimum liability due to obsolescence

Examples:

Major engine castings and purchased parts, steering gears, axles, radiators, batteries, prop, shafts, seats, springs, transmissions, wheels and drums, tires.

Approximately 82% purchased finished.

22.3% of Parts and 22.3% of Potential Shortages

22.3% of Total Cost

Group B

1. Medium Cost
2. Annual forecast
3. Reviewed Quarterly
4. Average banks
5. Control records show all transactions and balance
6. Normal follow-up
7. Monthly to quarterly shipments
8. Economic lot quantities
9. Controlled on max.-min. basis. Review order frequency
10. Negligible liability due to obsolescence

Examples:

Manifolds, pulley bearings, damper assemblies, camshafts, lifters, rod assemblies, valves, filters, gussets, hangers, cones and rollers, panels, horns, instruments, lights, floor mats.

Approximately 50% purchased finished.

74.6% of Parts and 74.6% of Potential Shortages

5.4% of Total Cost

Group C

1. Low cost
2. Annual forecast
3. Reviewed semiannually
4. Ample banks
5. Minimum control records ordering only
6. Normal follow-up
7. Quarterly to annual shipments
8. Economic lot quantities
9. Sealed minimums. Reorder when broken. Review frequency.
10. Negligible liability due to obsolescence

Examples:

Nuts, bolts, screws, washers, gaskets, covers, dowels, plugs, shims, pins, keys, springs, rings, tubes, retainers, brackets, spacers, clips, rivets, terminals.

Approximately 32% G.M.; 28% other. 60% total purchased finished.

because these are the parts that are constituting the largest share of your company's material costs.

Armed with this information, which is really only a shorthand method for identifying a company's "A" parts, you can then sit down with those in charge of your purchasing, engineering, and manufacturing departments to determine ways in which these parts can be purchased and inventoried more effectively. These are the parts that will benefit the most from implementing the purchasing techniques described in Chapters 3 and 4, and from the redesign decisions discussed in Chapter 5.

Understanding and implementing the 80-20 rule is only an initial shortcut toward implementing an ABC system, but it will provide immediate, impressive results. The next step, of course, is to classify all component parts into "A"s and "B"s and "C"s, and to undertake the more sophisticated techniques described in the remainder of this chapter. But for even this initial step to be successful, it is absolutely vital for you, as the top executive, to understand the concepts about sourcing described in the previous chapter so that you can understand and evaluate the information you receive from your department heads -- the purchasing chief in particular. It does little good for the head of the company to ask the purchasing chief whether they are following the many profit improvement procedures described in the previous chapter if the president lacks the background, expertise, or experience necessary to determine the accuracy of the purchaser's response.

Implementing an ABC System

An ABC classification system is, of course, only one technique used to classify raw material and component parts. (It can also be used for sales forecasting, as demonstrated in Chapter 6.) We happen to believe it is the best technique for most situations, but there are others. We'll discuss one of these alternatives, Material Requirements Planning (MRP), later in this chapter.

Regardless of what classification method is used, your goal should be to divide material and parts in such a way that those relatively few

items, representing the highest cost and generally the highest investment ("A" parts), are not the ones either left sitting idly or out of
stock for their full lead time. Conversely, the many low-cost items
("C" parts) should be purchased infrequently, since no matter how
many of them a company has on hand, they will not tie up large sums
of money. Of equal importance is that these low-cost items tend to
cause the greatest shortages. The reason is self-evident: the more frequently a part is used, the more likely it will run out. As will be discussed in more detail shortly, infrequent, large purchases of "C" parts
should eliminate the bulk of stock outages and still represent only a
very small portion of total inventory investment.

Translating this theory into an actual operation is really quite
simple. If a company with $10 million in sales purchases 75,000
2¢ screws six times a year, the money saved in inventory will not
nearly make up for the added cost in filing the paperwork every other
month, to say nothing of the serious risk of frequently depleting
inventory, thereby causing shortages and stockouts. Rather, a company's purchasing department should be expending its energies on
the more expensive parts -- the parts which when properly purchased
and controlled can result in major savings.

The initial step in ABC inventory control is to separate all
component parts in every product being manufactured, and classify
each part according to its cost, irrespective of whether that part is
made or bought. The classified parts should then be divided into
three groups: "A," "B," and "C." The most expensive parts should
be listed in the "A" group and the medium-priced items in the "B"
group. Into the "C" group should go all of the remaining, relatively
inexpensive, component parts. The cost of each part should be listed
within each of the three groups. This classification of parts must be
made for each finished product. The exception to this rule is for "specials," or items that are used infrequently. These items are treated
separately, in effect as a fourth classification.

Although reasonable arguments can be made for using either the
unit or the total volume system of ABC when determining if a part is

an "A," "B," or "C" part, we prefer using a hybrid approach that takes into account both unit value and total value. Our bias, however, is toward using unit value. For example, if a company uses one million screws at 2¢ each, our thinking is that each screw would be classified as a "C" part, despite the fact that the company is spending a total of $20,000 for them. In fact, we would tend to classify the part as a "C" even if we're using 10 or 20 million of a 2¢ part, although it could be reasonably argued that any part that is costing you $200,000 or $400,000 should be at least a "B" and perhaps even an "A". But we have found total value to be useful only when the same parts are used day after day on an assembly line in which relatively few finished models or products are manufactured. Unit value, on the other hand, works in all cases, has a much broader range of usage, and gives maximum protection against stock outage.

By studying Exhibit 4-2, one can begin to understand the form and substance of ABC inventory control. Note that in this example there are 231 parts costing less than 5¢, and 315 parts that cost between 5¢ and 10¢. Out of the 1,215 separate component parts used in the production of this model, 546 parts cost 10¢ or less and 849 cost $1 or less.

Most significant is that only 119 parts cost more than $25. These, then, are your "A" parts. There are 247 parts in the "B" group, costing from $1 to $25. There are 849 "C" parts, costing from less than 1¢ to $1. Exhibit 4-2, which is an actual example, clearly demonstrates that even in a model costing many thousands of dollars, the great bulk of component parts have relatively low unit values.

For this particular model, the "C" parts make up 70 percent of the total number of parts, the "B" parts make up 20 percent, and the "A" parts only 10 percent. This is a typical and reasonable ratio throughout most manufacturing operations.

Further analysis of Exhibit 4-2 reveals that while the "C" parts make up a large percentage of the total volume of parts, they make up a very small percentage of total costs. In fact, Exhibit 4-3, by taking

EXHIBIT 4-2: Breakdown of Parts by Cost

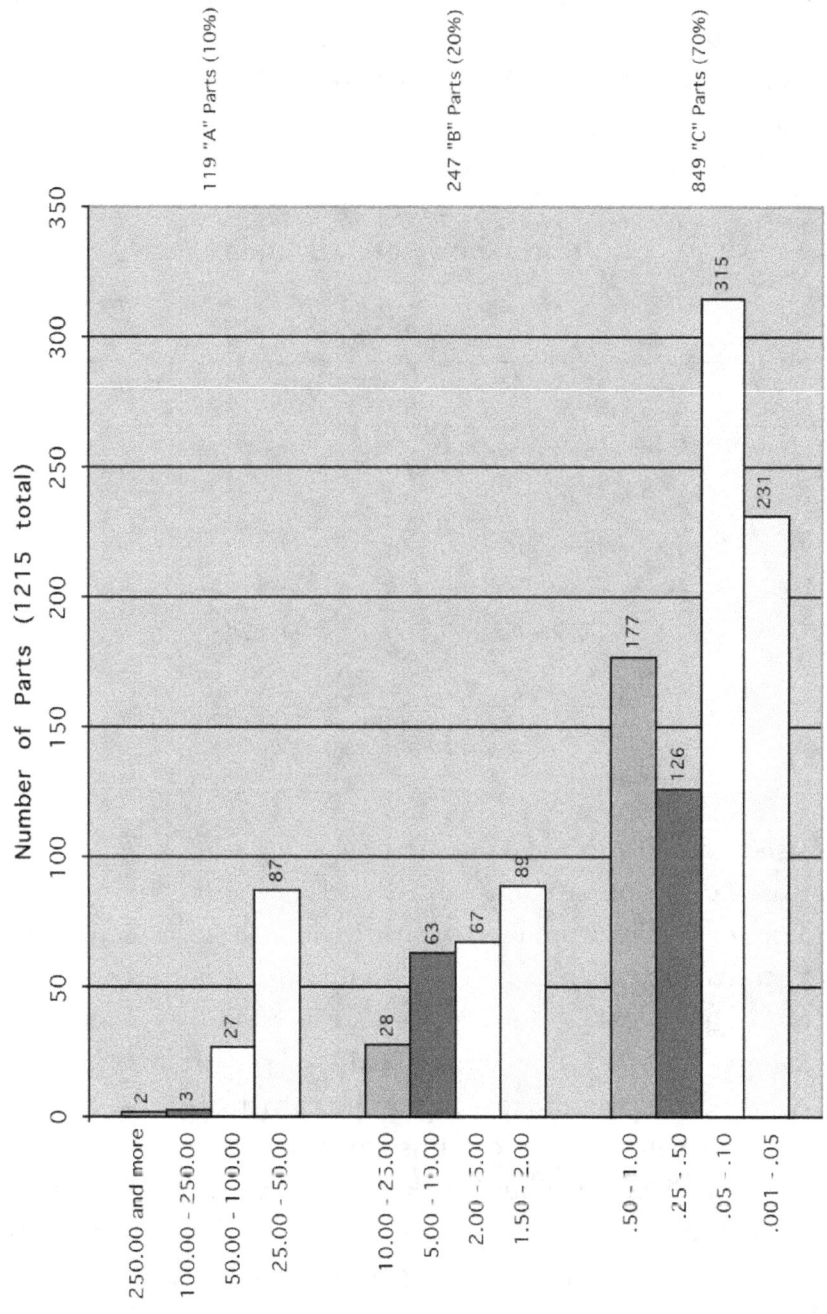

the median dollar figure for each category (the $.05-.10 category, in other words, is computed at $.075), demonstrates that in this particular model, the "C" parts make up only about 3 percent of total material costs.

Exhibit 4-3:
Cost Breakdown of A, B, and C Parts

"A" Parts			"B" Parts			"C" Parts		
No. of Parts	Median Cost of Parts ($)		No. of Parts	Median Cost of Parts ($)		No. of Parts	Median Cost of Parts ($)	
87 ^{5}	37.5 =	$3,262	89 ^{5}	1.75 =	$156	231 ^{5}	.01 =	$2.31
27 ^{5}	75 =	$2,025	67 ^{5}	3.5 =	$234	315 ^{5}	.075 =	$23.62
3 ^{5}	175 =	$525	63 ^{5}	7.5 =	$472	126 ^{5}	.38 =	$47.88
2 ^{5}	300 =	$600	28 ^{5}	17.5 =	$490	177 ^{5}	.75 =	$132.75
	=	$6,412		=	**$1,352**		=	**$207**

Total cost of all parts = $7,971
Total cost of all "A" parts = $6,412 (80%)
Total cost of all "B" parts = $1,352 (17%)
Total cost of all "C" parts = $207 (3%)

Variations Within the ABC Method

A breakdown of parts into an ABC classification will not look the same for any two products. Some items will be made up of more expensive parts than others, so the cutoff need not necessarily be $1 for "C" parts or $25 for "B" parts as in Exhibits 4-2 and 4-3. For example, a $1 part could be classified as a "B" part, or a $5 part as an "A," depending on the makeup of the particular items. In addition, "C" parts will normally comprise more than the 3 percent of costs that they did in Exhibit 4-3. Rarely, however, should they exceed 10 percent, so the conclusions demonstrated by our examples will be valid in most instances. Remember, a good rule of thumb is that 5-10 percent of your items will make up 70-75 percent of your costs,

86

20 percent of your items will make up 20 percent of your costs, and 70-75 percent of your items will make up 5-10 percent of your costs.

In some classification systems, "B" parts are eliminated altogether, and a distinction is made between "A" and "C" parts only. Other companies have a special "A +" or "AA" category for a few very expensive parts. As with virtually all the profit improvement techniques described in this text, the purpose is to enable you, as the chief executive, president, general manager, or other top-level person, to understand basic concepts so that you will recognize the importance of implementing these profit improvement techniques as part of a comprehensive program to maximize profits. You can then hire experts to implement them, or train your people in the technique, or do both.

Reducing Shortages

In addition to improving inventory turn, which frees working capital, transfers it into cash, and reduces costs by lowering interest expenses and obsolescence, another primary purpose of an ABC system is to minimize stock runouts and to maximize the speed with which a stockout can be rectified. Understand that regardless of your safety stock, stockouts can never be fully eliminated. This can be proven statistically since, as demonstrated clearly by Exhibit 4-4, when the level of safety stock increases, the probability line becomes asymptotic, meaning that it will never touch the 0 point on the graph's vertical line.

The probability of stock runouts varies per item and per product. Rates are generally based on forecast variances and volatility of usage. For example, in Exhibit 4-5 there are 12 truck models classified into 8 categories. Notice that each category has a different rate of probable runout versus forecast demand. If we provide a 40 percent safety stock for the type 20 model, the chance of runout is only 4 percent. If, on the other hand, the same level is provided for model 22, the possibility rises to 21 percent.

Exhibit 4-4:
Stockout Rate Graph

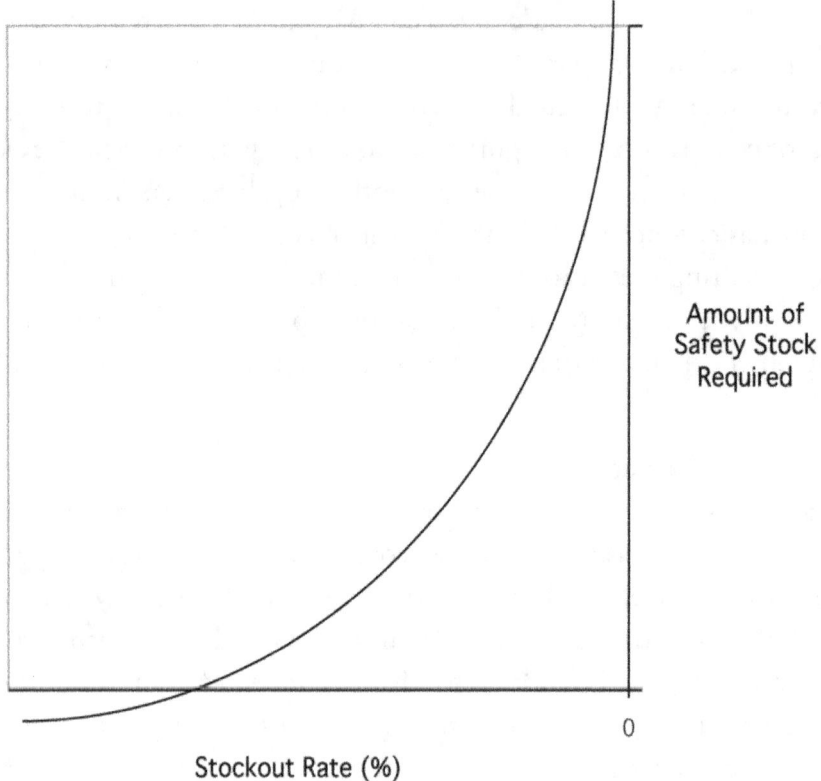

Amount of
Safety Stock
Required

0

Stockout Rate (%)

Exhibit 4-5:
Stock Run-out Probabilities

Inventory Level	Probability of Run-out[19]							
(% of Forecast Demand)	Model 20	Model 22	Model 22R	Model 50	Model 23D	Models 120-122	Model 226-406	Models 236, 236D, 536
100	50%	65%	55%	50%	58%	63%	66%	45%
105	40	59	47	44	53	55	60	41
110	34	53	39	38	47	49	55	38
115	25	47	31	33	42	42	50	35
120	20	41	24	29	37	35	45	31
125	14	35	18	24	32	29	40	28
130	10	30	13	20	27	23	36	25
135	6	25	10	16	23	18	31	23
140	4	21	6	13	19	13	28	20
145	2	17	4	10	15	10	24	18
150		13	3	8	13	8	20	16
155		10	2	6	10	5	18	14
160		8		4	8	4	14	12
165		6		3	6	2	12	10
170		4		2	4		10	8
175		3			3		8	6
180		2			2		6	5
185							5	4
190							4	3
195							3	2
200								

Material Requirements Planning

There are certainly other effective inventory control systems with which many companies have had great success. We just happen to favor our tried and true methods. The more you keep it simple, the more your entire organization will understand your goals and help

19. All these models are different trucks

bring them to fruition. Many companies, for example, use MRP -- Material Requirements Planning -- to schedule and monitor the use of components and other materials in a manufacturing operation. Like the more straightforward ABC system, MRP systems are today software-based. Also like an ABC classification, MRP is intended to meet three objectives:

- To ensure that materials and products are available for production and delivery to customers.
- To maintain the lowest level of inventory possible.
- To accurately and cost effectively plan manufacturing and purchasing activities and delivery schedules.

An ABC system can be used to clarify MRP. For one thing, it will ensure that you and your top people are fully aware, every day, of the risks of shortages and excess inventory. When you create a system yourself, and carry it around with you as a daily reminder, you are never far from understanding the current status of your operation.

While many companies have had great success implementing a sophisticated MRP system, be aware of a few potential drawbacks:

- Be extremely careful about the integrity of the data you are using. If there are any errors in what you are inputting, the outputted data will also be incorrect (garbage in, garbage out, in other words).
- MRP does not take *capacity* into account in its calculations. This means it will give results that may be impossible to implement due to manpower, machine, or supplier capacity constraints.
- Using an MRP system, you are required to specify how long it will take a factory to make a product from its component parts. The assumption is that manufacturing lead time will be identical each time the item is made, without regard to quantity or other items being manufactured simultaneously in the same factory. A manufacturer may have factories in different

cities or even countries. It is not helpful for an MRP system to tell you that you do not need to order a particular part because it is in stock at another factory thousands of miles away.

Regardless of what system you use, be certain that inventory is organized by the individual factory. At the same time, keep the lines of communications open so that, if practical, one factory can redistribute components to another in order to best serve the overall organization. Don't allow fiefdoms to build among factories or profit centers.

One final note about MRP. Material Requirement Planning can sometimes be confused with Manufacturing *Resource* Planning, mainly because they have the same acronym. Material *Requirement* Planning specifically defines a company's material requirements based on such factors as forecasts and projections, safety stock, a kanban system, or historical data. Manufacturing Resource Planning includes *all* aspects of resources that impact the manufacturing planning process, including not only materials, but also machinery, labor, set up, and raw materials.

"A" and "B" Parts

Every company is different, and the genius of the ABC system is its simplicity and flexibility. It can adapt to any kind of product mix. For "A" and "AA" parts, certain pragmatic rules apply to almost any situation:

- Keep inventories to a minimum.
- Keep tight controls, along with daily, detailed records.
- Make blanket purchase orders.
- Schedule inventory from your supplier so that it arrives at your plant frequently, perhaps as often as weekly. But even if a part arrives in monthly quantities twelve times a year, the turnover theoretically is twenty-four times annually for 70 percent of your investment. These parts should remain in work-in-process for the briefest time possible in order to hasten overall inventory turn.

For "B" parts, implement a modified program, combining the control characteristics exercised for "A" and "C" parts. As noted earlier, however, in certain instances some of these items listed as "B" parts might be categorized as "C" parts, or even as "A"s.

The need for "B" parts should be anticipated in an annual forecast, which should be reviewed quarterly in a check against usage. Inventories should be maintained at average levels, and all transactions (in and out), plus the inventory balance, should be recorded.

Shipments of the "B" items can be ordered on a monthly to quarterly basis, and the purchasing department should try to buy them in economic quantity lots. The order frequency should be reviewed periodically, keeping in mind that some "B" parts lend themselves to blanket orders with periodic releases for shipment.

"C" Parts

"C" items cause the greatest number of shortages and exact wasteful cost in time and energy unless adequate provisions are made. The first rule is to buy "C" items in quantity. It will do no harm to be "up to your ears" in them, and by ordering in bulk, the purchasing department will be dealing with its supplier from a position of strength, allowing negotiations for the lowest possible price. If you bring "C" parts in once a year, theoretically your turnover will be twice a year for 5-10 percent of your investment. If the parts are received twice a year, the theoretical turnover is four times, an equally acceptable turn for "C" parts. And should a standard "C" part stock out for any reason, it generally can be replaced quickly from a nearby supply house, thereby minimizing any disruption until a new shipment arrives.

The purchase of "C" parts can be made from an annual forecast reviewed no more than twice a year. Minimum records, for the purpose of ordering only, will be necessary. Remember also that obsolescence goes hand in hand with investment. By controlling "A" and "B" parts closely, the cost of obsolescence will be minimized. Assuming an obsolescence rate of 3 percent of your total inventory investment, obsolete "C" parts will be 3 percent of 5-10 percent, or between .15 and .3 percent. This will not cause any financial hardship, and besides, "C" parts tend to be standard items which your supplier will likely take back at a slight discount if you find yourself with an oversupply.

Manufacturers can afford to purchase large quantities of "C" parts infrequently, since they can be inventoried without tying up large sums of money. Buying them in bulk will permit the purchasing department to make the best possible, lowest cost, and highest quality, purchase. When "C" parts are stocked sufficiently, and a reliable control and delivery schedule is implemented for "B" parts, the purchasing department can appropriately concentrate on the handling, control, and turnover of the expensive "A" and "AA" parts.

Let's now go through a typical scenario that will demonstrate how easy it is to take delivery and keep a steady inventory of "C" parts, with minimal paperwork. A large quantity of, say, a certain type of cap screw, is received at the company dock. The bulk of the order is delivered to the assembly floor, while a predetermined safety quantity is simultaneously bagged and tagged and placed in an easily accessible storage area. When all the cap screws on the assembly floor are used, the safety bag is retrieved and sent to the assembly floor. The ticket attached to the safety bag is pulled, dropped into a box, and immediately sent to the purchasing department for reordering.

Only the most basic manufacturing discipline is necessary for this system to work properly. The worker who opens the safety bag pulls off the ticket and drops it into a box. From there the ticket is sent to the purchasing department, which in turn must know how long the safety quantity will last and therefore how quickly another large quantity will be needed. Today's equivalent of "pulling the ticket and dropping it into a box" and "sending it to the purchasing department" is entering it into the computer so the rest of the company can instantly see it.

Regardless of whether notification is given by hand or computer, the purchase should only have to be made once, or possibly twice, a year. The entire process is easily handled with a traveling requisition which, while simple, contains all necessary data.

This really describes a Kanban system. The Japanese word, Kanban, literally translates to *signboard* or *billboard*. Like an ABC system, it is simply a scheduling system that tells you what, when, and how much to produce.

The Savings

Now let's take a look at precisely what kind of savings can be expected through the implementation of an ABC program. This time we will use as an example an ABC classification where "A" parts make up 5 percent of the total number of parts and 75 percent of total cost; "B" parts are 20 percent by volume and 20 percent by cost; and "C" parts are 75 percent by volume and 5 percent by cost. Remember, without controls, shortages can on average be expected to correspond to these same percentages. In other words, if "A" parts make up 5 percent of the total number of parts, they can be expected to make up about 5 percent of the shortages. "C" parts make up 70-75 percent of both the total number of parts and the shortages, before controls are implemented.

In Exhibit 4-6 there is a normal monthly requirement for $1 million worth of inventory. This is the total amount required for parts that are being processed through the shop. With an average 3 ½ months of inventory, the average investment is $3.5 million, from which is subtracted a 5 percent obsolescence factor or, in dollars, $175,000. The average usable investment is thus $3.25 million.

By applying the ABC method to this same inventory requirement, the results are quite different, as can also be seen in Exhibit 4-6. While in Part I the work in process and finished goods are included, this has been adjusted in Parts II and III by using much lower turns for the "A" and "B" parts.

For items in the "A" group, constituting 5 percent of the parts, 75 percent of the cost, and 5 percent of the shortages, the monthly requirement is $750,000 (75 percent of $1 million). The average inventory required is one month's supply, so the average investment is $750,000.

Exhibit 4-6: Normal Inventory versus ABC Inventory

	Monthly Average Requirement	Average Inventory (Months)	Investment
I. *Normal Method*	$1,000,000	3.5 [20]	$3,325,000
II. *ABC Method*			
"A" Parts	$750,000	1	$ 750,000
(5% of items, 75% of cost, 5% of shortages)			
"B" Parts	$200,000	2	$ 400,000
(20% of items, 20% of cost, 20% of shortages)			
"C" Parts	$50,000	3	$ 150,000
(75% of items, 5% of cost, 75% of shortages)			$1,300,000
		Average Reserves	390,000
		Possible Obsolescence (2%)	33,800
		Average Turn (6.96)	1,723,800
III. *Savings*			
Total investment related to cash			$1,601,200
% of inventory released to cash			48.16 %
Cost of money savings (at 12%)			$ 192,144
Obsolescent savings (5% versus 2%)			$ 141,200

For items in the "B" group, constituting 20 percent of the parts, 20 percent of the cost, and 20 percent of the shortages, the monthly requirement is $200,000 (20 percent of $1 million). The average inventory required is a two-month supply. The average investment is thus $400,000.

For items in the "C" group, constituting 75 percent of the total parts, 5 percent of the cost, and 75 percent of the shortages, the monthly

20. Includes 5% obsolescence $175,000; represents a 3.32 times turn annually

requirement is $50,000 (5 percent of $1 million). The average inventory required is a three-month supply; thus the average investment is $150,000. With an average reserve of 30 percent, or $390,000, and possible obsolescence of 2 percent, or $33,800, the average investment totals $1,723,800, providing an average turn of 6.96.

Instead of an average investment of $3.325 million, as would be required under the normal method, the ABC method, by requiring only $1,723,800, avoids the expenditure of 48.16 percent of inventory, or $1,601,200 in cash. By reducing the obsolescence factor from 5 percent to 2 percent, there is a further savings of $141,200.

This reduction in obsolescence is possible because the high-investment items are watched more closely, and turning them more frequently eliminates, or at least greatly reduces, their numbers at a point where they might become obsolete, especially if an engineering change committee program is functioning effectively, as discussed in Chapter 5. It should be noted that, for purposes of simplicity, work-in-process (WIP) and finished goods have been ignored in this example. Work-in-process will be discussed in greater detail shortly.

Exhibit 4-6 conclusively illustrates that even in a small operation such as the one described, great savings can be realized through the implementation of an ABC inventory control program. The direct relationship between "A," "B," and "C" parts and potential shortages, as well as the inverse relationship to cost, provides a convincing argument that the small effort required to institute such a control program is extremely worthwhile. Among the many advantages of ABC are that it:

- Allows for the lowest possible inventory investment.
- Permits the fewest possible shortages.
- Minimizes placing salespeople in the position of having promised orders delivered late, or at least seriously late, due to waiting the full lead time for the replacement of stocked-out parts.
- Minimizes stockouts.
- Allows for speedy recovery from shortages.

- Encourages profit improvement through quantity purchases, including a system that permits blanket orders. (A blanket order is simply a confirmed long-term order for a specific good or service for a fixed period, quantity, and/or price.)
- Minimizes the cost of manufacturing parts in quantities and minimizes teardowns and setups.
- Results in faster and better customer service.
- Adapts easily to unexpected growth due to the reserves on hand in "B" and "C" parts and the strict control and blanket orders for "A" parts.
- Maximizes the efficiency of direct labor by proper scheduling.
- Minimizes the need for indirect labor and excess handling.
- Permits concentration on purchasing your most expensive parts as the most effective way to reduce costs.
- Reduces obsolescence.
- Simplifies record keeping.
- Forces management's attention toward accurate sales forecasting.
- Permits orderly (and frequently the simplest) shop functioning.

Shop Cycle Times

Elsewhere in this chapter we have repeatedly emphasized that steps should be taken to keep your "A" and "B" parts moving quickly through the production process and in small quantities, because they represent 90-95 percent of your investment. You would likely be surprised to learn the percentage of time the average part is worked on in a typical manufacturing facility. If you guess 1 percent, you are too high. Startling as this figure may be, see for yourself. Walk your shop and evaluate your in-process inventory. How long does it take a part to get through the plant? Then look at that part's process sheet. How long does it take to perform all the processes? It is a tiny fraction of the time that the part spends in the shop. Now you see why you don't want expensive "A" and "B" inventory sitting idle.

In order to simplify the discussion of the ABC concept, this chapter has thus far intentionally ignored work-in-process (or throughput time). Suffice it to say that taking steps to eliminate accumulations of "A" and "B" parts will result in smaller batches and more efficient movement of the parts between operations. In Chapter 8, we will see how computers have eliminated many "floor-to-floor" operations and have sped up the cycle and throughput time by combining a number of operations at one station. More efficient order-to-delivery strategies also have the benefit of improving customer service.

Experience Counts

More than any previous chapter in this book, the strategies explained here – ABC stratification, MRP, stockout charts, and probability variances -- require a certain amount of study to master. But in addition to statistical evaluation and analysis, a certain amount of judgment is also required. But the investment in time and focus to understand these techniques will pay rich rewards in a sharp reduction both in the risk of shortages, and your investment in the single largest outlay of your company's outgoing dollar. Let's just make one final review of the positive repercussions that will spread throughout your organization. A properly administered ABC system will:

- Reduce the need for complicated record keeping, including the need for sophisticated computer models that will likely not be understandable to all plant personnel.
- Prevent last minute expediting that makes it difficult to negotiate the best price or even locate the best product.
- Permit purchasing to make long-range buys at the best negotiated prices.
- Permit purchasing to concentrate on the more expensive "A" and "B" parts, issue blanket contracts, and schedule parts periodically.
- Minimize the extra setups and teardowns.
- Increase inventory turn.
- Free up working capital.
- Reduce obsolescence.

CHAPTER FIVE

REDESIGNING PRODUCTS FOR PROFIT

Some people now call the redesigning of products in order to maximize profits "Direct Material Optimization," or "investigating the manufacturing footprint." We simply call it product redesign. Whatever you call it, one of the greatest opportunities for profit improvement lies in the redesign of existing products. Not only can material, labor, and factory overhead costs be reduced, but the price and quality of your company's products can be improved so that they beat the competition.

As with most of the strategies discussed in these pages, the key is to remain diligent. Engineers and various manufacturing personnel need to be constantly on the lookout for creative ways to improve a product through a redesign, however slight. Products must be analyzed and reanalyzed with redesign in mind. Sometimes it's as simple as standardizing the different screws or joints on a particular product. Other times it's a complete overhaul made possible by new technology.

Despite its tremendous value, most companies place very little emphasis on product redesign, and therefore do a very poor job of it. That's a shame, because it is perhaps the most effective single way products can be continually improved, while simultaneously increasing profit margins. And it is a particularly valuable technique in this technological age, when failure to keep up with the latest design and functionality is a surefire way to make your products obsolete.

Why Redesign?

There are a number of different circumstances that can call for a product's redesign:

- Perhaps the cost of the product's raw materials has increased to such an extent that the finished product is no longer profitable.
- Or maybe a competitor has made important advancements and your company has not kept up.
- Some products face so much competition that a new redesign must always be on the drawing board.
- Sometimes the market has changed. Over the years automobile manufacturers have had to redesign their products due to the fluctuating demand for smaller, more fuel efficient cars. And most recently, they have undertaken a complete redesign effort in order to move away from the gasoline combustion engine and toward new technologies that will power electric, hybrid, and fuel cell vehicles.

Products that are no longer competitive in the marketplace need to be redesigned, but so do popular products. Why change a winner? For one thing, our knowledge in many fields is doubling every five to ten years, causing a steady decrease in the life cycle of the average product. For another, a popular product's volume can fund a redesign effort. Apple has perfected the redesign of a hit product.

Focus groups and direct customer input will often give you the insight you need. Sometimes only the inside working parts of a popular product need to be redesigned in order to maximize profits, while parts that a buyer sees and which appear in promotional materials need not be altered at all. In other instances, you will choose to alter a product's external appearance. Either way, a constant focus on redesign will cut costs, improve quality *and* profit, and keep up with artistic, technological, and state-of-the-art advancements.

Selecting a Product to Redesign

Often the best method of selecting products to be redesigned is to use a variation of the ABC method described in the previous two chapters. Just as a small percentage of parts make up a large percentage of material costs, you will also likely find that as little as 1 percent of your company's products provide 40 percent of sales, while perhaps 5 percent of the number of products provide 70 percent of sales. This 5 percent, designated as "A" products, should be analyzed for redesign on a regular basis.

Just as an ABC stratification system allows a company to align its priorities so that the most expensive items receive the greatest cost reduction attention, so, too, should a redesign program concentrate on the items that contribute most to the company's bottom line. A redesign program can then be further refined by linking some of the lower sales volume items to each of these "A" products and making families out of them. That way, some of the less popular models will be redesigned along the way. This is called "group technology," or GT, a manufacturing philosophy that emphasizes the grouping together of parts or products with a similar geometry, manufacturing process, or function. By achieving a higher level of integration between design and manufacturing functions, the goal is to reduce work-in-progress and lead times, thereby improving delivery performance.

Remember that in our ABC inventory control system described in Chapters 3 and 4, parts were classified according to unit value, not total value. This is not the case when choosing the products to be redesigned. Your company might sell only a handful of its highest quality, top-of-the-line items. While these may be expensive per unit, they may be "showcase" items, not contributing very much to your bottom line. Unless there is a clear trickle down effect, these products do not have top priority when it comes to redesign.

Product Redesign Committee

Every manufacturing company should have a redesign committee responsible for reviewing every proposed redesign. It should meet frequently and move quickly on accepting or rejecting each proposed change. It should also meet regularly with engineers and others in the company to encourage a climate in which redesign improvements are continuously sought.

The makeup of the redesign committee will depend on your company's particular organizational structure, but will usually include the head of purchasing, production, and inventory control, and the top manufacturing and engineering executives. Redesign decisions are so important that the product redesign committee should really be chaired by the top executive, or at least the general manager. Other team members will likely include a design, process, and tool engineer, and a foreman. Others may be added to the team at the request of the team leader.

No redesign, engineering change, or deviation, no matter how minor, should be put through without the approval of a product redesign committee. Only by getting input from a number of different key departments can a company determine how a particular change will affect its entire operation -- profits, pricing, procurement, obsolescence of inventory, and manufacturing capabilities. At companies where engineers are allowed to put through changes in parts and products at will, without any serious discussion concerning whether the change is actually necessary, a climate is created that leads to inventory obsolescence, surplus scrap, short runs, disrupted production schedules, unfavorable variances, higher costs, and poor customer delivery. These are the consequences of having no committee to review and approve redesign efforts.

The timing of a product redesign is crucial. If a change is made too late, the potential savings and the benefits to both the customer and to the company's competitive edge will be lost or delayed. But changes made too quickly can cause costly product delays and obsolete inventory. Of course, if product change is being made because of a safety issue, it will have to be made immediately.

Most times, a measured approach is warranted. During World War II, American industry manufactured a wide variety of war material as quickly as possible. One of the lessons learned was that most product improvements are not urgent and can be collected until a model change can be implemented. In the production of military airplanes, for example, improvements were being made almost daily, but the pilots needed planes to fly immediately. If the industry had waited to produce the perfect plane, the war would have ended before the first plane had left the plant. Instead, improvements were collected and made over a period of time.

One method a product redesign committee can use to anticipate the success of a redesign effort is a failure modes and effects analysis (FMEA). A proper FMEA helps predict potential failures based on past experience with similar products or processes, enabling the team to design those failures out of the system with minimum effort and expense. A FMEA can be used in various phases of a product life cycle in order to identify failure.[21] Sometimes studying the consequences of those failures is just as important as identifying the failure itself.

A Redesign Checklist

Ultimately, a product model to be redesigned will be selected on the basis of maximum potential improvement to the company's bottom line, verified by the accounting department. At a minimum, the product model review shall include an investigation as to whether:

(a) A material change would reduce costs.
(b) The number of subassembly parts can be reduced.
(c) Parts can be standardized.
(d) Maximum tolerances can be specified.
(e) Dimensions can be standardized.
(g) Test and adjustment procedures can be simplified.
(h) Process time can be reduced.

---

21. Failure, in this case, can be defined as any error or defect in a process, design, or product, especially those that could have an adverse impact on the customer.

Over the years, we have developed a checklist management can follow to make certain it is leaving no stone unturned in their redesign efforts. To get a complete picture of what goes into a redesign, take a look at Exhibit 5-1. You can see by the extensiveness and detail of the list that this effort must be taken seriously by your company's most creative, knowledgeable executives.

Exhibit 5-1:
Design to Cost Checklist

1. Are all the specification requirements necessary or desirable?
2. Is the hardware's function clearly understood?
3. Does the design provide only what is required in the specifications?
4. Is the design as simple as possible, and does it provide only essential functions?
5. Has standard or existing hardware been utilized to their fullest extent?
6. Are tolerances and finishes substantially contributing to the cost of the product?
7. Can alternate materials be used to reduce costs?
8. Can the design be changed to minimize use of special tooling or equipment?
9. Have newly developed manufacturing techniques been considered for their potential cost advantage?
10. Is there a standard item that can be satisfactorily substituted for this part?
11. Is there a design change that will lower the cost of the item?
12. Would the cost of the hardware be reduced if the customer provided standard hardware and materials and performed processing operations themselves?
13. Can the entire subassembly be made smaller, reducing material?
14. Is it possible to buy preassembled parts from the supplier?
15. Can more parts on a particular job be made of the identical raw material?

16. Can the part and tools be designed to reduce scrap in machining?
17. Can the need for complicated equipment requiring continuous scrutiny and maintenance be eliminated?
18. Have the suppliers' engineers been given sufficient facts and pressed for suggestions that would produce equivalent performance at lower cost?
19. Should minor changes suggested by the supplier that would afford lower-cost material be considered further?
20. Are parts obtained in the best economical lot sizes?
21. Is there any part of this item that can be more economically produced by different methods of casting, forging, extruding, or other processes?
22. Are there any test or qualification requirements that appear unnecessary?
23. Are there any other ways to save weight, simplify the part, or reduce the cost?
24. Is there a standard item that can be satisfactorily substituted for this part?
25. Are all tolerances used in actual practice the same as on the drawing?
26. Can the design be changed to eliminate or simplify the operation?
27. If part is a casting, can it be made lighter by additional coring?
28. Does the design of the part present difficulties when casting?
29. Can a form cutter perform two or three operations on a certain job at one time more economically than performing the operations separately?
30. Could higher-cost tooling be justified by increasing order quantity?
31. Could the supplier perform additional work on the material that would make it better suited for its use?
32. Can the machinability of the material be improved by heat treatment or in any other way?
33. If a more expensive material that was easier to machine were substituted, would there be a savings?

34. Could the parting of the patterns be changed to eliminate a machining operation on the casting?
35. Could molded or cast parts be substituted to eliminate machining or any other operation?
36. Can the design be changed to eliminate excessive loss of scrap material?
37. Can extruded material be used?
38. Is the supplier performing an assembly operation on a part or material that your company later dismantles?

"Not Invented Here" Syndrome

One of the biggest challenges in product redesign is overcoming pride of authorship, sometimes called the "not invented here" (NIH) syndrome. Just as it is difficult for parents to look objectively at their own offspring, it is equally difficult for an engineering department to look objectively at one of its own products.

Redesign changes can be made in order to improve a product, or to reduce costs. They are distinct and separate functions, even if in the end one type of redesign often helps the other. Redesign Committee members should be on the lookout for engineers who insist on making a "quantum leap" improvement simultaneously with redesign cost improvements. That is often inappropriate.

There are several possible ways to avert the NIH syndrome. They all are intended to give the redesign responsibility to someone other than the engineer who designed the original product.

1. Hire an outside firm to take charge of all redesign efforts. If this option is chosen, be certain to review carefully the capabilities of the person assigned to product redesign and be absolutely specific in the instructions for improvements to profit, quality, and performance. This outside firm will still have to work closely with your own redesign committee.
2. Find the maverick engineer in your own organization who doesn't run with the pack. Provide a separate office and

a specific assignment, and turn this engineer loose. This approach can be very successful in certain circumstances -- to achieve maximum standardization, for example.

3. In some cases you will find total objectivity in your organization. This is unusual, but conceivable if you have the right kind of people. Even in this instance, however, do not allow the same engineers who originally worked on the selected product to have primary responsibility for its redesign.

You may be surprised at the results of a proper product redesign effort. Savings will be obtained, and at the same time quality and performance will usually improve. An initial redesign will often provide ideas for a second redesign of the same product at a later date. Company morale and esteem quite frequently will also be boosted. Employees deservedly feel a sense of satisfaction and pride when their company's products are continually being improved. It also gives sales personnel a new talking point with customers, and increases their enthusiasm and confidence.

Value Analysis

Like many of the strategies described in this text, value analysis has evolved into a variety of sophisticated techniques developed and implemented effectively by top consulting companies. Function Analysis System Technique, for example, or FAST, is one of the many evolutions of the value analysis process that permits people with different technical backgrounds to effectively communicate and resolve issues. But these newer techniques have at their core a strategy that has been around since at least the 1940s of applying a function analysis to the component parts of a product. Value analysis supports maximizing profits by relating the cost of components to how they contribute to the basic function of a product. It defines "basic function" as anything that makes the product work or sell. Basic functions are also defined as those that cannot change, as opposed to secondary functions that can be modified or eliminated to reduce the cost of the product or to improve it in some other way.

The goal of a value analysis is the possible substitution of one part or product for another. In no way does it matter whether the physical characteristics of an item remain identical, as long as the item performs the necessary function with equal or improved efficiency.

A textbook example of value analysis is a large hotel chain whose supply of nine-ounce water glasses has gradually been depleted and needs replacing. The hotel may not have bought water glasses for several years, and when it contacts its supplier it finds that nine ounce glasses are no longer a stock item. The hotel can buy the glasses if it insists, but they will be inordinately expensive.

Another supplier, however, manufactures a ten-ounce glass that is substantially less expensive because they carry it as a stock item. The ten-ounce glass serves exactly the same purpose as did the nine-ounce glass. Through a very simple value analysis process the hotel chain determines it should buy the larger, equally efficient water glass.

Value analysis is usually more complicated than that, of course. To take the same example, other hotels have replaced their water glasses with ones made of plastic. Before that kind of decision is made, a variety of factors need to be taken into account, including the initial cost of both the glass and plastic items; the cost of breakage, sterilization, and packaging; and consumer preference and expectations. Environmental factors also come into play.

Value analysis involves an organized system of techniques and practices that should be an integral part of the manufacturing operation. It cannot be completed successfully without input from the purchasing department, which is the department most aware of the various cost-reducing options, and engineering, which should have some creative ideas of their own about other, more out-of-the-box solutions. Value analysis is so important that a training program for key personnel is usually warranted.

Exhibits 5-2 and 5-3 represent two simple examples of how value analysis principles might be applied.

Exhibit 5-2:
Value Analysis Case Study

A company manufactures fire-fighting equipment, including a small wall-mounted fire extinguisher. The bracket used to affix the extinguisher to a wall has for many years been made of metal. At the recommendation of the company's value analysis team, the bracket is reduced in size and is now made of plastic, at a savings to the company of 50 percent of the entire cost of the bracket.

Exhibit 5-3:
Another Value Analysis Case Study

On certain products, an ongoing value analysis process will continually make improvements. In the 1950's, the exterior moldings on automobiles were attached to the body of the car by a variety of metal clips. The clips were heavy, and attaching them required drilling into the side of a car, locating the clip, fastening it to the fender, and then finally attaching the molding to the clip. The process was time-consuming and costly.

The first improvement was to standardize all the clips so that every automobile used the same set. A few years later the metal was replaced by plastic, and the clips became lighter and significantly less expensive to produce. The next step, sometime in the early sixties, was to eliminate the fastener altogether by applying the moldings with a double adhesive strip. This did away with the labor involved in drilling the holes and aligning and applying the clamp, and replaced the plastic clamps with less expensive strips of adhesive. The latest innovation has been to substitute the adhesive strip with an even less expensive epoxy, which is also easier to apply.

The metal strips on a thirty-year-old car look the same as they do on today's models. The difference between how they are fastened cannot be determined by the naked eye, but there is a large manufacturing difference, and a major cost savings.

Make-or-Buy Decisions

Any consideration of how to maximize profits involves a tough but elementary decision: to make or to buy. Is it more profitable for your company to manufacture a part than it is to buy it?

Again, this is a job for the purchasing department. Other departments should be involved, to be sure, and someone from manufacturing or engineering may be put in charge. But your purchasers are most likely to have access to the key information that will compel a decision. From the very beginning, purchasing can make a vital contribution by asking the current supplier to identify his breakdown of material and labor costs, as well as by ascertaining the lowest possible outside price. Only then will it be possible to compare in-house costs to that of the outside supplier.

Exhibit 5-4:
Make-or-Buy Case Study

A company purchasing unfinished components in four Pacific Rim countries and doing final machining in the United States decides to evaluate its in-house machining costs. It wants to compare the gross margin of these components if it began buying them completely finished from the individual countries.

By having the components machined in the Pacific Rim, the purchasing agent, in concert with manufacturing, is able to negotiate a price for the completely finished components that increases the company's profit margin by 20 percent. What's more, these products are low margin items that demand signifi-cant machining time, so the company's factory is able to pick up some much needed machining capacity.

Exhibit 5-5:
Another Make-or-Buy Case Study

A sporting goods company manufactures top-of-the-line baseball gloves. Like any quality item, the gloves are quite expensive. They are made of quality leather, and hand sewn in the United States. They retail for between $200 and $300.

While these gloves are important for this company's prestige, as well as for its overall sales strategy, they are priced out of the reach of most consumers. In order to satisfy the broader market, a less expensive glove is also offered.

An engineer collects the cost of raw materials, transportation, and labor from a number of sources, including the purchasing department. The analysis by the make-or-buy team determines that the minimum cost of producing an inexpensive glove is $50, but marketing announces that in order to be competitive and to attract the targeted consumer, the glove has to sell for $49.95. That leaves no room for profit.

The purchasing department requests bids from outside manufac-turers, mostly from low-cost countries around the globe. It finds a line of quality gloves it can purchase for $25, so the decision is to buy rather than to make. The analysis doesn't stop there, however. The purchasing department takes this opportunity to make an in-depth analysis of each component of the $50 cost in order to determine why its in-house costs are so high.

Variable versus Fixed Costs

In any make-or-buy decision, total costs must be investigated, as well as each individual cost. For example, if a machine part is purchased from an outside source for $50, the total outlay of the company is $50 in direct exchange for a given part. If, on the other hand, the company decides to make the part itself, all the elements that make up the direct costs of producing that part must be investigated. In this case, direct costs refer to the material, labor, variable, and semi-variable costs that directly relate to the part.

In this example, let's say your make-or-buy team informs you that their analysis projects an in-house cost of $40, with the following breakdown:

Material	$24
Direct labor	6
Applicable non-fixed overhead	10
Total	$40

Obviously, the savings here are substantial, but this uses variable, or non-fixed, overhead. If we calculated the cost using full overhead, including fixed, it might look like this:

Material	$24
Direct labor	6
Applicable fixed overhead	15
Total	$45

Even using full overhead, the saving is still $5, so it passes the first "make" test. In other words, the numbers make it attractive to make this part in-house. There is one more factor to consider, however. We have assumed that factory space, machinery, and knowledge all currently exist to produce the product or part in question. If it requires the addition of any capital or heavy expense item, then the calculation must be carried further to determine real payback.

The importance of taking into account fixed overhead costs becomes even more evident when a company considers stopping the in-house production of a product in favor of purchasing it from the outside. The fixed overhead of $5 will not go away, so the cost of purchasing the product is actually $55, not $50. Variable, or non-fixed, overhead can be saved once the product is purchased from a third party. Fixed overhead, which generally includes depreciation of capital equipment, manufacturing supervisory personnel salaries, and shop supplies like rags and cutting tools, cannot.

The decision whether to make or buy is, of course, not a difficult one when the cost differential is substantial. If, for example, the in-house cost is $40 and the outside price is $50, simple arithmetic demonstrates that it is advantageous to make the part rather than to buy it. Yet often a kind of twilight zone occurs when the cost straddles the outside purchase price. Using our $50 part as an example, suppose that the cost using material, labor, and non-fixed overhead comes to $48, but the cost using full overhead is $52. In this case, let's say the non-fixed overhead is $8 and total overhead is $12.

Assuming the machinery and manpower are available, serious consideration should be given to bringing it in-house. The reason is straightforward. Of the $12 overhead, you will absorb about $10.64 -- all of the non-fixed ($8.00), and approximately two-thirds of the fixed ($2.64). Your inventory investment technically should not increase if properly controlled, and your own workers would be kept busy.

Our view is that all things being equal, we prefer to make a product rather than buy it, as long as the existing knowledge, equipment, and space are sufficiently available. In our experience, once a product is moved into our sphere of influence we can improve its contribution to the company's bottom line by implementing the various profit improvement strategies discussed in this text. Without this kind of confidence, however -- without having absorbed the lessons in this book, for example -- it may not be wise to bring a product in-house when the cost analysis has proven to be ambiguous. It is a judgment call. Remember, however, for every product you take out of a plant, you increase the overhead for all your other products, which may reduce or even eliminate their profitability as well.

Product Elimination

At some point your financial manager, sales manager, or some other executive may recommend eliminating a product that, at least on the surface, seems to be losing money. Although there certainly are circumstances that require the elimination of a product or even an entire line of products, a top executive should be extremely wary of such requests. In our experience, four factors have usually not been taken into account when the elimination of a product is requested:

1. Are you certain that all your decisions are based on accurate cost data? Pay particular attention to how overhead costs have been assigned. And be sure that standard costs have not misled your analysis. (See Chapter 7 for a complete discussion of the dangers of using standard costs.)
2. Be certain that an in-depth analysis has been made to determine whether a product redesign could substantially lower material, labor, or overhead costs.
3. Is there a readily available replacement? If not, factory overhead, selling, and G & A costs for the eliminated product will have to be spread across the remaining product lines.
4. Does the company have a plan for the orderly elimination of the product or product line to keep obsolescence and inventory to a minimum? Ask yourself the same question for the equipment or plant involved.

Product Extension

There will be times when it is advisable to add new products, and even to enter entirely new business areas. This is particularly appropriate for companies in mature industries which can identify new ventures that have significant growth opportunity. Ideally, any new area should complement existing expertise.

Exhibit 5-6:
Product Extension Case Study

A $30 million company manufactures elevated work platforms for the fire protection industry. It is a mature market, and the opportunities for growth are slim. Company management recognizes that they must diversify in order to survive. A marketing study determines that elevated work platforms, used in the construction industry and in industrial plants for plant maintenance, are poised to become a growth industry. Of equal importance is the fact that the product has many similarities to the products already manufactured by the company. A certain in-house expertise already exists, especially in hydraulic design.

Before introducing any new product, the company rents the top two or three machines in this field in order to understand the competition. Within thirty days, the engineering, marketing, and service departments have analyzed the three machines and prepared a detailed report. In one machine the team finds a faulty braking system which could allow a runaway condition when on a slope or grade, not a very attractive characteristic for a unit that carries a worker thirty feet in the air. To counteract this problem, the other two machines have spring-set, electric release brakes. This solves the braking problem, but causes abrupt stops, also not too comforting to the person perched thirty feet high.

A product redesign solves the braking problem by installing a double braking system, consisting of an automatic spring applied brake, actuated only when the operator removes his or her foot from a foot-operated safety switch on the platform, then steps on a hydraulic foot brake, similar to the brake on a car. Other improvements are also designed, including the installation of a 48-volt battery system which, compared to the competitors' 36-volt system, adds one-third more energy to the battery pack and roughly the same increase to operating time. A direct-drive connection between the turntable and the chassis is replaced by a rotation system, which provides positive but smooth rotation and prevents any possible movement from an external force. Still another improvement is the use of a chrome plated pivot pin with Teflon bushings. This eliminates the need for lubrication, which, according to the study conducted by the company's service department, customers frequently neglected to perform anyway. A rheostat control provides an inexpensive but effective variation of speeds to all function movements. And finally, the prototype is outfitted with 33 feet of working height, two feet higher than its tallest competitor. The design team also creates an attractive design.

The marketing department is convinced that it has developed a better machine than what is presently on the market, but also knows that it is going to cost more to build. One suggestion is to accept a smaller margin, but that is immediately rejected. There is no point building the machine if it cannot be sold profitably. The list price of the newly designed product is subsequently placed $2,000 higher than that of its nearest competitor.

Two prototypes are built. The first is given to the division's engineering department for testing in the field. After an evaluation, improvements are made and various components are tested in order to determine which ones work best. The second prototype is painted and given to the sales department so a marketing effort can be initiated. Sales literature, publication advertisements, direct mailers, and presentation materials on DVD and online are prepared, and the unit is shown off at trade shows. The comments from suppliers and potential customers are then applied to the final design.

On the surface, the odds might seem to be stacked against this company. It is a newcomer in a very competitive elevating work platforms business. In fact, there are already 8 U.S., 4 Japanese, 2 German, 2 French, 2 English, 1 Finnish, 1 New Zealand, and 1 Australian manufacturers of competitive boom products. Even more alarming is that the company's product is more expensive than any of its competitors.

This company has an ace in the hole, however. It may sell the most expensive product, but it also is confident that its product is worth the higher cost; that important improvements have been made and it is therefore the best quality machine available.

In ten years this company increased its sales by 500 percent and its profit margins by significantly more than that. It became number two in the industry, with a 24 percent share in the United States, and is poised to enter the international market-place with a product that has a proven track record.

Summary

The profit improvements that can be realized through a comprehensive and proper redesign effort fluctuate widely, depending on the extent of the redesign. The standardization of three different screws into one will obviously have a smaller impact than the redesign of a compli-cated control valve that reduces both the number of moving parts and the size of the valve's body. Both are important changes, however. Be assured that product redesign can save substantial sums, and there-fore can have a dramatic effect on profit (assuming the savings are not given away unintentionally, as will be discussed in Chapter 7). Conscientious redesign should be able to reduce your costs by at least 10 percent, and often significantly more than that. The bulk of the savings will likely be achieved in labor, material, and overhead.

CHAPTER SIX

Smart Sales Forecasting

The importance of accurately forecasting future sales would seem to be self-evident. A company needs at least a fairly accurate idea of how many units of its product can be sold. If too many units are manufactured, inventory investment and carrying costs increase, as does obsolescence. If too few products are produced, sales are forfeited, customers alienated, and sales personnel frustrated. Without reasonably accurate sales forecasts, maintaining effective inventory control is almost impossible, which creates havoc in both good times and bad.

Accurate sales forecasts based on precise, relevant data provide the foundation necessary to avoid or mitigate shortages on the one hand, and stock overruns on the other. It can also help identify growth opportunities.

Yet, in the typical American manufacturing operation, sales forecasting is little more than guesswork. Usually no one bothers with even the most elementary relevant data, like third party forecasts for the overall economy, trends for the particular industry in question, or the company's own historical data. This is a shame because reliable sales forecasting is achievable within limits, and is not particularly expensive.

One reason for *inaccurate* sales forecasting is an overreliance on the opinions of salespeople in the field. This is a fundamental error made by a great many sales managers, and, in turn, by many presidents and chief executives too. While input from salespeople should certainly be one factor in a comprehensive study, it is unfair to expect them to supply figures on which production schedules will be based. By nature and by training, sales personnel are optimists. They would much rather have full shelves than empty ones no matter how quickly or slowly they are able to move their products.

Salespeople are the ones on the front lines, however, and their intuition and instincts, based on their experience funneled through the head of the sales department, do have an important role to play in forecasting sales. An estimate based on personal experience is always an important addition to established data.

After receiving their projections, ask salespeople to comment on the trend lines for their particular product areas. A sales department will often be in the best position to factor in all sorts of information, such as which lines or models:

- Will receive the most marketing (advertising, special promotions, discounts, etc.) in the period for which forecasts are being made.
- Will face the stiffest competition.
- Are scheduled to be phased out, downgraded, or replaced.
- Can be categorized as "A" products, meaning that they comprise the bulk of your company's sales.

Seasonal and Historic Trend Lines

Begin with historical product data complete with trend lines adjusted for seasonal changes. Then extend these lines to the coming year. Other data that should be investigated include forecasts for the industry in which the company operates, forecasts for the economy as a whole, and correlative indices, selected because traditionally or historically they parallel or otherwise have a relationship to the company's own markets.

These figures, weighed by their significance and estimated accuracy, will then be measured against the historic trend line of the sales of the company's key products or product lines.

No sales forecasting can be expected to be 100 percent accurate, but making an educated guess is certainly better than ignoring sales forecasting altogether. Ensure it is reasonable by:

- Checking industry forecasts.
- Trying to learn what competitors are planning.

- Studying U.S. and international forecasts.
- Examining the phase of the current business cycle and the expected phases for the forecasted period.
- Consulting trends and projections in correlative indices.
- Working from a historic trend line that has been established from the company's own sales records.
- Giving consideration to seasonal patterns and adjustments.
- Developing individualized pressure curves.

Exhibit 6-1: Trend Line of Seasonal Indices Compared with Undisciplined Forecasts

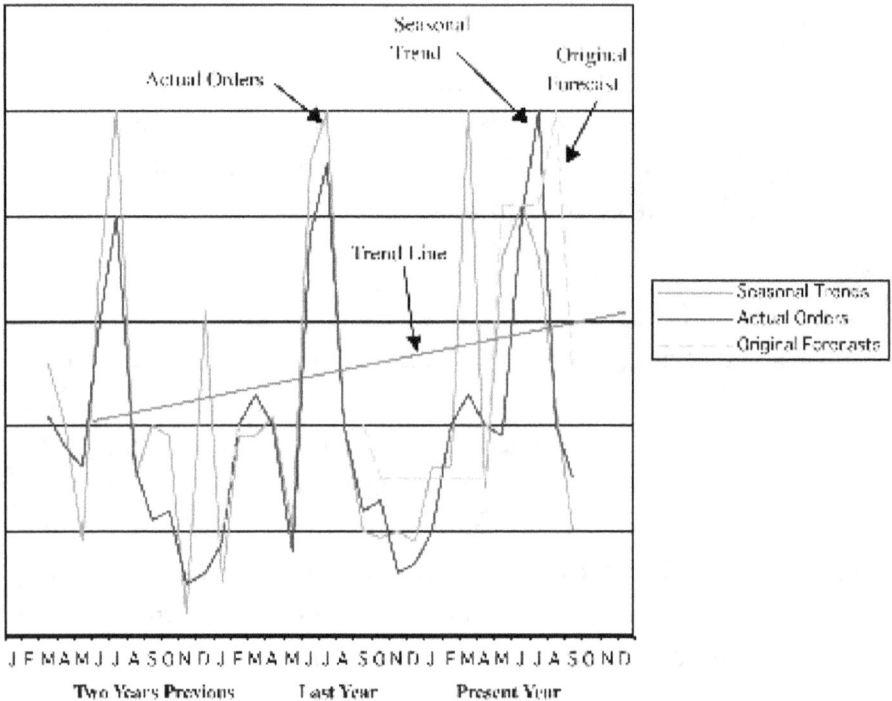

Study the graph depicted in Exhibit 6-1, which compares a typical company's actual sales for the previous two years with the present year plus projections. Note that there is a rising multiyear trend line which must be calculated into future sales estimates. In this instance, the head of sales offered a good forecast, adjusted seasonally. The calculated seasonal trend was extremely accurate for all three years and better than the raw forecast.

Creating a chart showing a historic trend line with seasonal fluctuations can be a good first step toward bringing a degree of accuracy to the vital assignment of estimating future sales. Such a chart can then be combined with other historical information. The state of the economy, for example, as measured by the major economic indicators has a profound effect on virtually any kind of business. If there is a drop in the trend line for the gross national product (GNP), the person charged with forecasting a company's sales should check back to see what happened to sales the previous times the GNP slowed by the same rate. Such statistics as the unemployment rate, retail sales, and unsold inventories should also be considered.

Comparisons can also be made with correlative economic indicators that have demonstrated their visible relationship to the sales of your particular company. In some cases, the appropriate data will be obvious. A manufacturer of component parts for kitchen appliances, for example, will want to measure the figures for building construction, housing starts, real estate sales, and the home mortgage market. Other appropriate data might not seem so obvious. It may be that the same indicators used for a company that manufactures kitchen component parts are also essential in forecasting sales for lawn mowers or laundry detergents. New car sales are used by many department store retailers in forecasting their sales of dry goods and hardware. One of the most important initial sales forecasting tasks, well before any actual projections are made, is to determine the most reliable economic indicators that, though perhaps seemingly unrelated, presage or foretell sales trends in your industry.

Studying these economic indicators can help with other decisions besides just sales forecasting, such as when it is prudent to intensify or cut back on advertising, when to extend credit to customers, and even when infrastructure expansion is justified. Whenever possible, historic trend lines should be developed for each product or product group.

In setting up your own correlative studies, you may want to ask for professional help from a consultant, or better yet from the economics department of a local university. Once established, the data can be maintained internally, or a university-based economist can supply quarterly figures for the correlative indices you have deemed most relevant. While much of this data is available free on government web sites, a third party can format and analyze the data according to your particular needs.

Four Basic Elements of Sales Forecasting

Every sales forecasting analysis should include four different kinds of economic data. Every top executive should understand each of them – at least enough to be able to ask the appropriate questions of internal or consulting experts, and to understand the information provided.

- *Trends* are the long-term, long-range movements of a series of economic data. They have little relationship to the month-to-month changes that take place, and they manifest their direction slowly.
- *Cycles* are of shorter duration. Though generally of unspecified length, they are usually featured by alternate periods of expansion and contraction. Their duration may vary widely, as may their intensity in either direction.
- *Seasonal variations* occur within a certain period of the year and recur at about the same time and to approximately the same extent from year to year. Changes in intensity are generally in agreement with the long-term trend line.
- *Irregular variations* are the result of unforeseen or non-recurring events that have an economic influence. A strike in a key industry, for instance, might cause an irregular variation.

Time Series Analysis

A time series analysis is a statistical technique that separates the cyclical, trend forces from other types of forces, particularly those due to seasonal factors. Although the analysis might not apply directly to a manufacturing operation, it is used to forecast retail sales, which in turn has a significant impact on many manufacturing operations.

For retailers, the seasonal influence on each month of the year provides an essential guide toward making sound decisions about how to behave in the short term. A time series analyses takes into account indicators like disposable income, gross national product, expenditures for consumer services, the consumer price index of both goods and services, and consumer spending for both durable and nondurable goods. It can help a company adjust its pricing, inventory, purchasing, and the size of its sales force.

Pressure and Rate-of-Change Curves

A pressure curve, often called a rate-of-change curve, is simply a graph showing the percent change in the twelve-month moving average of any series of monthly numbers. At a glance, a company's situation can be compared to its situation at the same time twelve months earlier.

This method of identifying stages of the business cycle is also sometimes called cycle forecasting. While you may well need an expert versed in this particular procedure to establish and analyze the appropriate series of pressure curves for your company, even a cursory examination of the pressure curve depicted in Exhibit 6-2 will demonstrate the potential value of this important technique.

Exhibit 6-2 depicts a twelve-month pressure curve of a $17 million industrial company superimposed alongside a graph of that same company's sales volume on a twelve-month moving total over a ten-year period. The pressure curve has been calculated by dividing each twelve-month sales total by its level the year before in order to obtain an index figure relative to one hundred. In other words, when the pressure curve is at the one hundred mark, it is a signal that sales volume for that twelve month period is equal to what it was a year earlier.

Exhibit 6-2: Sales Volume Pressure Curve

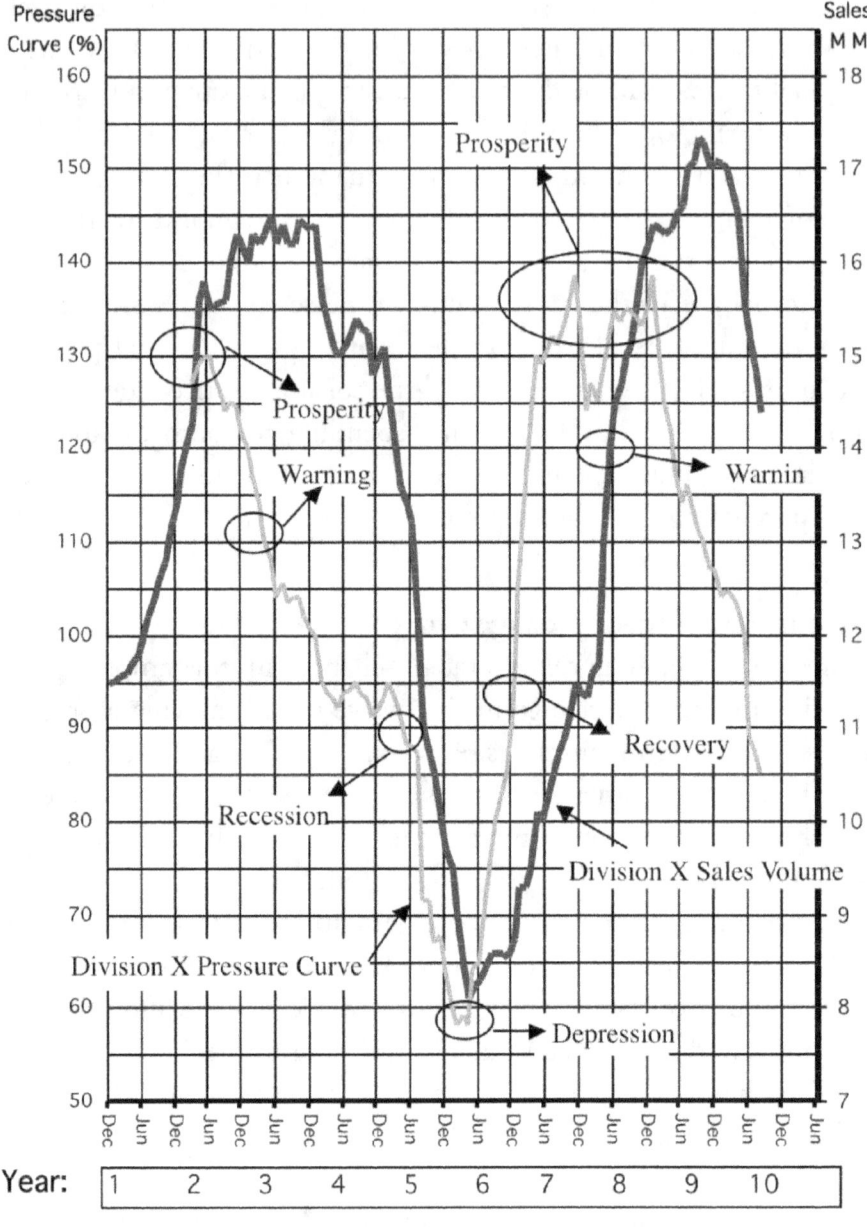

The pressure curve clearly shows that three times during years two to ten, this company experienced sales at the same level as the year before: December of the third year, December of the sixth year, and April of the tenth year. This can be confirmed by looking at the sales volume graph alongside the pressure curve.

Now let's use the graph to predict future sales. Look at the middle of the ninth year. Note that the pressure curve is in the midst of a decline. Sales have continued to increase, but at a decreasing rate. This should have served as a warning that this company would shortly be experiencing a decline in sales. You can see that this began to occur about a year later, early in the tenth year.

In order to make the most effective use of pressure curves, a company should go beyond plotting its own sales volume. Pressure curves can be created from other internal indicators, like bookings, inventory levels, and operating expenses. In fact, comparing a pressure curve of operating expenses alongside a graph showing sales volume will provide a good indicator as to whether the company is sufficiently decreasing operating expenses to meet an anticipated decline in sales. Often a company finds that operating expenses have remained stagnant or have increased even in the face of a recessionary dip in sales. Likewise, when the sales pressure curve is in a recovery and growth mode, you will know that it is appropriate if expenses increase.

Pressure curves can also be used to plot external indicators that have been found to correlate with your particular company, such as the index of consumer sentiment, housing starts, or automobile or retail sales (see "Seasonal and Historic Trend Lines" section earlier in this chapter). Laid side by side with pressure curves that plot internal data, external indices will frequently predict the direction and amplitude of short term sales.

Six Phases of the Economic Cycle

By plotting a company's performance over a number of years and identifying dependable cycles, a pressure curve allows a company to recognize the six phases of the economic cycle, each of which is labeled in Exhibit 6-2. A company can then act accordingly, depending on which phase is approaching.

The **growth phase** occurs when conditions are expected to improve. Note that in Exhibit 6-2, this company experienced a growth phase during almost all of year eight. This is the time when inventories should be maintained at high levels, salespeople should be added, new product lines introduced, advertising and sales promotion increased, and sales training programs accelerated.

The **prosperity phase** occurs when a company is at its pinnacle for that cycle and the gains on the pressure curve become narrower. For the company depicted in Exhibit 6-2, this occurred toward the end of the seventh year and during all of year eight. Although inventories should be maintained at high levels during this phase, a company should also begin to plan for leaner days. This will include launching marketing programs in anticipation of lackluster sales of at least some product lines, freezing certain expansion programs that have been scheduled, and establishing policies for rationing to customers in case shortages suddenly occur.

The **warning phase** occurs when business is still increasing, but at a decreasing rate. As a rule, this leveling off should occur for three months before this third phase is properly identified, such as during year nine in the Exhibit 6-2 example. Once a company enters this phase, inventories should immediately be reduced, advertising cut back, and marginal products eliminated.

The **recession phase** occurs when business begins to fall below the previous year's level – beginning in May of year ten in our example. During this phase a company should:

- Reduce operating expenses as much as possible.
- Question the necessity of new activities.
- Review and adjust prices.
- Tighten customer return policies.
- Further reduce advertising, training programs, hiring, and executive travel.

- Continue to maintain tight control on quality and customer service.

The **depression phase** occurs when business is still decreasing, but the rate of decrease appears to be bottoming out. Often the losses on the pressure curve will be erratic for twelve months or more. During this phase a company should:

- Reduce most advertising.
- Continue a reduction in sales force.
- Continue to reduce and balance inventories.
- Streamline management, perhaps by combining offices, plants, or divisions.
- Seek to improve quality even amidst other cutbacks.
- Begin to think about the next recovery period.
- Begin to plan for long-term growth, sales training programs, and a search for top-level people.

When you are certain you are at the bottom of the trough, also make sure "C" part banks are well stocked, "A" and "B" parts are well-covered with blanket orders, and your sources have sufficient stocks on hand to supply you quickly. Load up on your safety stocks and keep your key suppliers in position to increase supplies quickly. Adjust your lead times outwards before they actually hit.

During the **recovery phase**, business will still be below year-ago levels, but the pressure curve will show that the tailspin has slowed. Manufacturing operations are in a difficult situation under these circumstances. Since sales volume has not yet forecasted the upturn, once the recovery phase does begin, the purchasing department is often unable to source their required parts because lead times have stretched quickly, safety stocks have begun to become depleted, and control systems have started to fail.

The recovery phase is probably the most difficult phase to recognize, but once it has been identified, this is the time to be aggressive, so that when the growth period comes around again you will be ready for it. Work force reductions should be halted, sales training programs jump started, new product lines introduced, and advertising and sales promotions renewed. In other words, an overall growth strategy should be developed in order to exploit the business upturn that is about to begin.

With experience, you will no doubt develop your own methods for identifying the different phases of the business cycle. One trick is to gain insight from the type of assignments management consulting firms are receiving. When a recession is in progress, they tend to get a heavy preponderance of two types of assignments -- cost reduction and sales and marketing programs (*How do we stay profitable?* and *How do we reverse declining sales?*). During recovery stages, they typically land a lot of inventory and production control jobs because manufacturing is unable to keep up with sales. Another clue is that assignments are more difficult to come by at the top and the bottom of the business cycle because businesses are generally undecided as to which way the economy is going to move, so they are not certain what their needs will be.

Summary

No one should expect sales forecasting to be totally accurate right down to the last model unit. However, armed with the data discussed in this chapter, as well as estimates by internal sales staff, a forecast by model number or product line for the upcoming period, usually accurate to within 10 percent, should be possible. Only then will a company be able to plan inventory, production control, and schedules successfully. Not only will accurate sales forecasting eliminate costly shortages and surpluses, but the resulting improvement in your inventory control system will prove to be an additional tool in your effort to maximize profits.

CHAPTER SEVEN

PRICING YOURSELF INTO PROFITS

The sad irony of many profit improvement programs is that the gains realized after so much hard work and effort are forfeited by a faulty or misunderstood pricing system. Months and countless hours may be spent:

- Restructuring a company's organization.
- Setting realistic goals through macro and micro ratio analyses.
- Instituting smart sales forecasting.
- Establishing a proper set of priorities.
- Redesigning products.
- Taking a variety of measures to make certain procurement procedures are operating at maximum efficiency and profitability.

But unless top management is aware of the pitfalls of pricing, a company faces the imminent danger of losing part of, all, or in some cases even more than these profit improvement techniques have attained. You may not even be aware of what has happened until it is too late -- until you take a look at the bottom line and can't understand why the substantial savings you worked so hard to realize did not translate into an increase in profit, and why in some cases your profit percentage actually fell.

Pricing pitfalls are particularly dangerous during periods of high inflation. Inflation can move so fast and be so far reaching that it simply cannot be offset by profit improvement techniques alone. For several years now, the inflation rate has hovered between 1 and 3 percent, but it won't always be that way. Don't be lulled into a false sense of security. Even when the consumer price index is rising by only a few percentage points annually or less, the price of certain raw materials vital to your manufacturing operation can suddenly rise much more rapidly than that. Your costs affiliated with personnel will also continue to rise. Raises based on seniority, as well as taxes and employee health insurance plans, seem always to increase at a pace higher than the overall inflation rate. The price of gas and electricity will probably do likewise.

No matter what the official inflation rate, over the long run it is suicidal not to build added costs into the price of your product. Before you know it you are squeezed by higher costs on the one hand, and stagnant prices of *your* products on the other, and you may not be able to suddenly pass price increases along to the customer. As a result, your cost improvement strategies are being used just to maintain past margins, not necessarily improve them.

The days of protecting customers from price increases for sixty or ninety days should become a thing of the past. Instead, purchasing departments should build and maintain a weighted index of "A" parts and discuss changes regularly with the company's top executive. Only by closely monitoring those costs can an intelligent decision be made about when and how much to raise the prices of finished products with "A" part content.

We have found that the best method for determining if your company's pricing structure is out of whack is to keep a careful eye on the cost of materials as a percentage of sales. As soon as this percentage begins to increase, this is an indication that your company's pricing structure has not kept pace with inflation. This is a very simple and quick indicator, and is virtually foolproof. Some manufacturing and sales personnel may argue that their product mix has changed, but only rarely will products change so drastically and so rapidly as to justify such an excuse.

The Danger of Standard Costs
Even without inflation, a faulty pricing system can, within a matter of months, negate the benefits of a comprehensive profit improvement

program. The most common and most insidious way this can happen is if your pricing relies on standard costs. Standard costs should be called the opiate of managers because it dulls their senses. Rarely do they understand or appreciate their true ramifications. They are probably the greatest enemy of profit improvement. We recognize that this is an iconoclastic position, but bear with us as we develop the logic behind it.

Financial managers and other accounting personnel use standard costs in order to price inventories and tabulate profit and loss statements. But these standards are often also used, incorrectly, to *price* the items. When the standard cost of a particular part is estimated, it is invariably based on the cost of the item the last time it was purchased. But if the purchasing department has not bought that item for a year or more, this standard price will be too low. Prices of materials can change monthly.

When standard costs are too low, the final cost of the completed item will also be too low, and profits will soon disappear. The answer is for your controller or financial manager to continually update prices received from the purchasing department. Even this solution, however, will not be successful if priced off standards.

Standard prices are often set in late summer or early fall, several months before the calendar year in which they will be used. Even if the purchasing department gives the company's financial manager current prices, rather than the price from the last time the item was purchased, the standard price might easily be too low by the time they are actually put into effect. Similarly, the standard price, even if accurate on the first of January, could easily be off base by the end of the year.

In order to achieve any degree of validity, standard prices need to be continually adjusted, or even set higher at the beginning of the year in order to take into account estimates for the upcoming twelve months. Remember, the price of your most important materials will often rise more rapidly than the government-reported consumer price index.

The price of materials is not the only cost that needs to be monitored. Negative variances will also occur if a company's accounting department incorrectly estimates other standard costs, such as labor and overhead.

Negative Variance

All too often, standard costs are set with the full knowledge that almost immediately after the start of the new year, there will be negative variances in material, labor, or overhead (or all three). A negative variance is the difference between a financial plan and an outcome that results in a less favorable profit than expected. In this case, it refers to a cost of goods and other expenses that will surely be out of date by the time the product is sold. If you price off standard costs with full knowledge that negative variances will occur early in the year, you cannot attain your budget and profit goals.

Adjustments need to be made in order to recognize these variances. Prices should be raised not only to offset past increases in the cost of materials, but also to offset projected cost increases during the coming year. As soon as sufficient "A" part material price changes are experienced and an approximate level of change can be ascertained, prices can once again be revised in order to maintain a positive variance. Obviously, any price increase has to be sensitive to what the market will bear.

The Insidious Giveaway

So far we have not even discussed the most important reason why standard costs, as used in much of industry today, are such a serious deterrent to good management and reasonable profits. The most frequent and most damaging way a faulty pricing mechanism negates the positive results of profit improvement strategies occurs literally every day and has very little to do with inflation. All too often the savings realized through a profit improvement program are deducted directly off the standard cost of the item. Then a constant markup is used to adjust the sale price. That reduces or eliminates the benefit of any cost savings you have worked so hard to attain.

We call this damaging effect of standard costs "the insidious giveaway." Study Exhibit 7-1, which depicts a product that was cost reduced and repriced, only to lose all the savings, plus part of the product's original gross profit. Note the cost breakdown: $50 has gone for materials, $20 for labor, and $60 for overhead. The total cost of producing the item is thus $130, on top of which are added selling and general and administrative costs, plus a 5 percent profit margin, for a selling price of $173.30. The financial manager has arrived at this final selling price by marking up the standard cost of sales ($130) by 33.3 percent ($130 x 1.33 = $173.30). Selling and general administrative costs are $34.70 (20 percent of $173.30), and pretax profit is $8.60 (5 percent of $173.30).

Exhibit 7-1: The Pitfalls of Pricing

	Original Item Cost and Selling Price Using a 33.3% Markup	Subsequent Cost Reduction with the Profit Protected by No Standard Cost Change	Change in Price and Profit When Old Markup (33.3%) is Applied to Revised Cost
Selling price	$173.30	$173.30	$120
Costs Material	$50	$40	$40
Labor	$20	$10	$10
Overhead	$60	$40	$40
Total	$130	$90	$90
Selling and General and Administrative (20%)	$34.70	$34.70	$34.70
Total Cost	$164.70	$124.70	$124.70
Pretax Profit	$8.60 (5%)	$48.60 (28%)	- 4.70 (-2.7%)

Now the financial manager looks at the new cost figures after a profit improvement program has been implemented. Through the implementation of an ABC inventory classification system and other innovative purchasing techniques, material costs have been cut by 20 percent, reducing them from $50 to $40 per item. Ratio analysis, lean manufacturing, redesign, and process improvement have saved 50 percent of the cost of direct labor, reducing that cost from $20 to $10 per item. And finally, plant consolidation, elimination of some indirect labor, resulting fringe savings, and increased plant utilization based on proper make-or-buy decisions have garnered a 33 percent reduction in overhead, reducing that cost per item from $60 to $40. Now the total cost of producing this item is $90 instead of $130 -- all because of the success of our profit improvement program.

First let's take a look at what happens when the benefits of cost reduction are passed on to the company in the form of profit. Looking at the second column in Exhibit 7-1, we see that selling and general and administrative costs have remained at $34.70. We have done nothing to increase or decrease these cost areas. If we keep the final price of the item at $173.30, our profit has risen to $48.60. Profit as percentage of sales has jumped from 5 to 28 percent. In other words, the hard work that was put into the comprehensive profit improvement program has paid off in the form of increased profits (both dollars and margin), and has made the company more competitive by not being forced to keep raising prices, although it still can if the market warrants it.

All too often, however, something very strange happens with profit improvement savings. Take a look at the third column in Exhibit 7-1. The financial manager (or, more likely, one of the clerical personnel), unaware of what has been accomplished through profit improvement strategies, has taken the revised $90 standard costs and applied the same factor for markup (33 percent) that was used in the past. The financial manager comes up with a final selling price of $120 ($90 x 1.33 = $120).

The financial manager, however, neglected to realize that selling and general and administrative costs have remained at $34.70, and that the effect of a $120 selling price is the total elimination of profit. In fact, the company will lose $4.70 on each item it sells, or a swing of $53.30 per item.

Put another way, the profit improvement program has eliminated $40 from the cost of the item, but the pricing structure has cut $53.30 from the final price of the item. The financial manager, and possibly the sales manager, by doing what they perceive to be their duty, have taken away more than profit improvement efforts have saved on every unit sold. All the benefits and more have gone to the customer, plus the expenses, plus the cost of G & A. Your profit improvement program has been totally neutralized.

We have seen this scenario over and over again. Cost figures are turned over to the financial manager, who is allowed to set final prices in collaboration with the sales manager. These are the individuals in your organization in a position to give away all that your profit improvement program has gained. Prices are set mechanically off revised standards without regard to protecting or improving profits, and frequently in a perfunctory manner by clerical personnel. They may think that it is in everyone's best interests to pass along the impressive cost reductions in the form of lower prices. Worse yet, they probably do it without even realizing it. The result will be the same: to price your company right out of black ink and into the red.

This scenario might sound ludicrous. It is. But it occurs, and it occurs widely and frequently. It probably occurs in your company, at least to some extent. Cost reduction will eliminate profit unless the pricing arm of the company recognizes and understands what the rest of the management team is doing. If a constant markup factor is applied to standard costs, and it is revised every time costs have been reduced, this scenario becomes self perpetuating. Pricing and standard costs must be completely divorced from one another if cost reductions are to be protected and profits improved.

Ultimately, it is the president or chief executive officer who must be responsible for making certain that the controller or other financial executive does not set prices using unyielding formulas. Pricing policies and techniques must be administered carefully and policed by the head of the organization. The key personnel involved must be educated about both proper strategies and the ramifications of improper procedures. Standard costs can be used for internal purposes, of course, but pricing needs to be a separate and divorced function based on other norms. To do otherwise invites disaster.

Whose Fault Is it?

Most of you are familiar with the old saw, "Sure we are losing money on each item, but look at our increase in volume!" Sales personnel and sales managers will often fight against price rises, arguing that sales will suffer. But if you are selling at a loss there's no point being in business in the first place. What's more, sales personnel are notoriously poor predictors of the effects of a rise in prices. Nevertheless, a poor pricing policy should by no means be blamed on sales personnel or the financial manager. It is the job of salespeople to sell. They have little way of knowing how much they need to charge for an item in order for the company to make a profit.

As for financial managers, they simply receive notice that the cost of an item is, say $90. They mechanically multiply this by a factor of 1.30 or some other figure to cover administrative costs and profit, and mark the price of the item at $120. Financial managers usually have no way of knowing that the item sold for much more the previous year, that the cost has been cut due to an intensive profit improvement program, and that by changing the price to $120 the benefits of the company's efforts have actually been negated, and the product has been priced to lose money.

A Solution to the Insidious Giveaway

The dangers of using standard costs threaten your profit margins month after month, year after year. If a favorable variance is maintained for twelve months, and then the pitfalls of pricing are once again ignored, the accounting department will give away your cost reduction savings in the second year by lowering the standard cost. Remember, as always we are using the terms cost reduction and profit improvement interchangeably – the glass half full or half empty, depending mostly on your personality.

Some of the following tricks used to avoid the trap of standard costs may seem heretical, since you are not using the costs on the data sheet given to you by your accounting department. But a study of the preceding pages, as well as a little work of your own with a pad and pencil, should convince you that your pricing system needs some kind of built-in protection. Pricing for sales is different than pricing for inventory and shop control.

One solution is to not report profit improvement savings to the financial manager at all, forcing prices to be set off false standards. Favorable variances can be deferred in inventory and passed to income during inventory evaluation once a year. An inventory adjustment can then be made annually. Other companies simply raise their prices periodically regardless of profit improvement efforts, using old unrevised standards adjusted for inflation but not cost reduction.

Once the situation is fully recognized and understood, a compromise between a price reduction and a maximization of profits can often be reached. In this way, some of the savings realized through your profit improvement efforts will be passed on to the company in the form of increased profits, and some to the customer through a price reduction if this is deemed wise or acceptable, particularly if it will boost your market share. Your decision will depend on the situation.

No matter what decision you make, someone in your company should be responsible for making certain that profit improvement efforts serve to increase, rather than decrease, profits. Returning for a moment to Exhibit 7-1, the financial and sales managers could have taken the $40 that was saved by cost reduction and deducted it from the original selling price of $173.30. This would have resulted in a new selling price of $133.30, a substantial reduction in price that would have provided a good competitive edge, while at the same time permitted the company to receive the same amount of money in profit and for selling and G & A expenses as it had the previous year. The amount of pretax profit would have been the same -- $8.60 -- but the percentage of profit would have increased from 5 percent (8.60 divided by $173.30 = .05) to 6.5 percent (8.60 divided by 133.30 = .065). The other measure that should be considered is return on assets, which will vary from company to company.

The solution just described passes all of the cost reduction savings on to the customer. Thirty-one percent ($40 divided by $130) of the original cost of the item was saved through cost reduction, and profit was only increased 1.5 percentage points. It may very well be that this company would want to make more of a compromise between the 5 percent profit depicted in the first column in Exhibit 7-1 and the 28 percent in the second column. Perhaps the company would decide to split the $40 increase in profit ($48.60 − 8.60 = $40) evenly between profits and the final price, which would mean a $20 increase in profit and $20 reduction in price. In that case, the price of the item would be $153.30 and profit $28.60. This would serve to simultaneously increase profit, as well as your product's price competitiveness. We like that solution.

There are, of course, an infinite number of ways in which cost reduction savings can be divided between profit and price. The amount of profit your company will make on any one particular item will depend on a variety of factors, most prominent of which are your existing profit percentage, your competition's price for the same or similar item, and your company's desire to increase its share of the market. If, for example, a product was redesigned because it was beginning to lose money, most if not all of the cost savings may have to go to profit. If, on the other hand, the competition is selling virtually the identical item at a substantially lower price, or if your company has put a priority on increasing market share, then most of the cost savings probably should go towards a reduction in the final price of the item, assuming the item is price sensitive.

Regardless of how you decide to divide the savings that you have gained through your profit improvement program, what is most important is that key company personnel are aware of the entire situation, and make their decision from a position of knowledge and strength, rather than from confusion and ignorance. As with an ABC inventory control system, you have selected a suit of clothes off the rack; now it has to be tailored to your specific needs. And in this instance, it will be a delicate tailoring job indeed.

Exhibit 7-2:
A Pricing Pitfall Case Study

PIWB Inc. has an item that cost $100 to manufacture, and is being sold with a conventional markup of 66.66 percent on the cost of sales, at $166.60 (16.60 x $100 = $166.60). Profit improvement techniques cut $10 from the cost -- from $100 to $90. The controller passes the figure along to the sales manager, who in turn prices the model at $150 -- its $90 cost multiplied by the 1.66 factor.

The result is that having saved $10 in production costs, the sales department has given away $16.70 on each model sold. It not only knocked out the dollar that had been saved, it took away an additional $6.70 from profit.

But wait, it gets worse. Further investigation reveals that sales personnel are giving quantity discounts that have absolutely no relationship to the savings that had been realized by the profit improvement program. Sales personnel are taking orders for 10,000 quantities with a standard gross margin of only 13 percent. It also turns out that some of the buyers who placed orders for lots of 10,000 are actually taking delivery of only a few hundred. In addition, groups of individuals are joining together to order in 10,000 lots, but receiving deliveries of their share at diverse locations.

PIWB Inc. is also marking up its product by 40 percent of its cost rather than as a way of attaining a 40 percent gross margin. A 40 percent gross margin requires a 66.6 percent markup (or a multiple of 1.667), while a straight 40 percent markup on cost yields only 28.5 percent (or a multiple of 1.404). For example, if an item costs $60 to make, with a 40 percent margin it *should sell for $100, since 40 percent of $100 equals $40. A 40 percent straight markup on that same $60 item would put its selling price at $84, providing a $24 gross profit or 28 percent of sales. This probably would not cover the cost of selling and G & A, much less leave any room for profit. The item would most likely sell at a loss. This company has a lot of work to do before its pricing mechanism complements, rather than battles, its profit improvement efforts.*

Summary

Say you manufacture a part with a standard cost of $10, which you sell at wholesale for $20. Using our profit improvement techniques, you reduce costs to $9, and then use the same markup to sell the product for $18. You are giving away $2 for every dollar you save!

The fault does not lie with sales personnel. The ultimate responsibility for maintaining a sensible and effective pricing policy should fall on the top executive, followed by the company's designated financial officer, both of whom need to keep pricing under continual surveillance. A cross-functional, multi-discipline team should also be constantly reviewing your company's pricing strategies.

Pricing is the last line of defense both for your profit improvement program and against the effects of inflation of your key materials. Establishing the correct prices for your products in order to ensure you make a profit is the final step, after all of the strategies espoused in this book have been put in effect. If it is ignored, all that has been gained and more will be dissipated.

Make no mistake about it. Pricing is an extremely difficult area to control. There is no foolproof system. The best a company can hope to do is to keep its shop costs and standards totally divorced from its pricing mechanism. They are two entirely different areas and should be treated that way.

CHAPTER EIGHT

Labor Standards, Work Sampling and New Machinery

The best way to make certain labor costs are not out of line is through an effective standards program. When properly maintained, a standards program can yield substantial savings, but the timing of its implementation is also extremely important. If standards are installed too early, before unnecessary costs have been eliminated through other, more elementary techniques, you will only be applying standards to a bloated organization. When confronted with an overweight elephant, the entire animal must be trimmed before scientifically engineered standards can effectively be introduced. But don't delay too long. If you wait until your company is running at optimum efficiency, which is invariably a moving target, the standards may *never* be implemented. There is no such thing as a "perfect" manufacturing operation, so the timing will be a matter of judgment.

Production Standards

The most important information you can take from Exhibit 8-1 is that a company with no labor control standards at all can assume its labor costs are approximately 100 percent excessive. That means that every day you will be getting less than four hours of work for eight hours of pay, and direct and indirect labor costs, which together can constitute 15-20 percent or more of the sales dollars (with fringes added), will be about twice as high as necessary.

Exhibit 8-1 Spectrum of Labor Cost Excess

TYPE	Labor Cost Excess, %				
	0	25	50	75	100
No Control					
Gross Estimated Standards					
Historical Standards					
Work Sampling					
Engineered Standards–Day Work					
Engineered Standards - Incentive					

Exhibit 8-1 also shows the range of labor excess according to each type of production standard. Note that an old style work sampling can reduce excess to 30-50 percent, and in some cases even less. Proper engineered standards can bring it down to 10-15 percent in a non-incentive system.

As usual, a dose of common sense can also be added to the mix. Non-routine functions, for example, can be expected to have a lower performance or efficiency level than a routine operation. Construction workers are probably less efficient than direct labor in a factory. But regardless of the type of operation, be assured that major savings in the cost of labor can be realized by implementing production standards.

What is a Production Standard?

A production standard is the time required to produce a desired quality, product, or service:

- By an average, qualified, experienced worker.
- Working at a normal pace.
- Following the standardized method.
- Using the prescribed equipment.
- Operating at standardized feeds and speeds.

- Taking the allowed personal, fatigue, and delay allowances (typically about 15 percent).

There are basically three ways in which standards can be determined:

- Gross estimated standards are simply an educated estimate of how much production will be completed by a machine, function, or operator in a specified period of time. With gross estimated standards, excess labor costs can still be expected to average between 75 and 90 percent.
- Historical standards can be used for an operation that has been conducted in previous years. The company knows approximately what to expect. Historical standards will reduce excess labor 50-75 percent.
- By far the most effective ongoing standards program is engineered standards, which can cut labor excess to 10 percent or less.

Work Sampling

While definitely old school, work sampling is actually the most straightforward approach to reducing investment in direct labor and machinery. Through the application of random observations, it obtains facts about human activities and machines. In a work sample, a job is sampled at random intervals to determine the proportion of total time spent on each particular task. By sampling the frequency and effectiveness of activity at the various work stations within a plant or an office, you can pinpoint levels of productivity and inefficiency by both workers and machinery.

Most managers have only a vague idea of how their employees spend their time. Work sampling can identify the types of activities staff perform, and the amount of time they spend on each activity. Armed with this information, managers can make decisions regarding allocation of staff and activities, thereby increasing productivity. Work sampling can also identify jobs or work conditions most susceptible to the most prevalent types of work-related injuries, which, if undetected, lead to higher workers' compensation costs, decreased productivity, and increased turnover.

While costing a small fraction of a regular continuous standards program, work sampling can provide a reliable estimate of the efficiency of your shop floor and the utilization levels of your various pieces of equipment. It can provide valuable information concerning three vital aspects of an operation:

1. Percentage of time employees are working.
2. Rate at which employees are working.
3. Utilization of machinery.

There are some who refer to work sampling as "ratio delay studies," but we reject that term for two reasons. The first is obvious: we are not really looking for delays, but for production enhancements. Second, we are observing and sampling work, not idleness, even though the results *will* tell us the frequency of idle status and the sources of delay. Work sampling serves as a substitute for work standards, and provides a general appraisal of your existing standards system and equipment utilization. In addition to being used to divide work operations into its various components, it can also be used to obtain data used as the basis for wage incentives, work measurements, and performance ratings.

Most companies no longer include work sampling in their repertoire of profit improvement tools, and we do not expect full-fledged work sampling operations to suddenly spring back into vogue. We do believe, however, that understanding its elegance -- that by simple observation you can pinpoint weaknesses in your operation – is a vital part of understanding where your inefficiencies in labor and machinery lie, and the most obvious ways to make improvements. A simple work sample has also become much easier to implement, as computers and sophisticated software have eliminated the tedious, error-prone task of manual data entry using stopwatches and note-pads. The time it takes to work sample an operation has been reduced from weeks and months to a matter of days, allowing a business to implement changes and solutions much faster. Computerized results also mean that a work sampling operation can easily be customized to suit specific investigations.

We consider work sampling to be the old school equivalent of the Japanese Kaizen/Kanban philosophy of sitting in the center of a circle in order to observe what's going on in your company. Sometimes there's no better route toward methods improvement than watching, scrutinizing, and analyzing what you see in front of your very eyes.

Engineered Standards

An engineered standards program contributes to improved productivity through three specific benefits:

- Process improvement. Methods are improved through a better use of station layout, operation motion sequence, proper tooling, and machine feeds and speeds.
- Time utilization. Time is utilized more productively because its use is being measured and accounted for.
- A more consistent work pace. Work pace becomes more consistent because workers know what is expected of them.

Engineered standards can be implemented through the use of either predetermined time data or time study data. The primary difference is the length of time of the motions (or elements) that are measured. Time study data is concerned with comparatively large segments of time, all of which can be measured by a stopwatch. Predetermined time data measures much shorter periods, called micro motions, which are much too short to be measured by a stopwatch.

The time-and-motion technique uses an observer to record exactly how much time is being devoted to each task. This is much more labor intensive than work sampling because observers must follow the subject continuously for extended periods of time. It is also more precise.

The primary problem with a simple time study is that when dealing with the comparatively long elements of time made necessary by stopwatch measurement, a worker can easily beat a company's standard by making minute changes within the long elements of a task. Time studies, therefore, become loose and inaccurate in just a few years, and union contract language can make it difficult to make changes.

With a predetermined time standard, however, the worker's reach or grasp or other minute change is made up of many micro motions. If a manager can show that the worker has changed the micro motions, management can change the standards, since the method has changed and, hence, the standard. This has been well established by arbitration rulings.

Predetermined time data requires the recording and documenting of physical motions and the application of a predetermined "normal time" to each motion. By developing a "library" of work elements and times, and selecting those elements that apply to a specific product or task, it is a natural progression to engineered standards. While the installation of a library may require the help of a qualified consultant, it can be maintained internally by most any experienced supervisor. The introduction of engineered standards involves the highest engineering skills, and hence the highest development costs. But once all other profit improvement techniques have been employed, this is the ultimate cost control tool.

Engineered standards are thoroughly acceptable to unions and should be part of any mature, well managed company. They have another advantage that many people do not perceive or understand. Armed with the data developed by engineered standards, a company can price a new product before it is ever manufactured. Before the first unit is built, its place in the competitive marketplace can, with reasonable accuracy, be determined.

New Plants and Equipment

While establishing profit improvement priorities, new plant and equipment is almost never on the top of the list. Most of the profit improvement strategies already discussed, including ratio analysis, various purchasing techniques, product redesign, and the coordination of a sensible pricing mechanism -- are remarkably inexpensive to implement. Purchasing new plants and equipment, on the other hand, is extremely costly. While upgrading to the newest technology may indeed reduce costs and improve productivity, it will also substantially increase overhead through depreciation charges, and if done in large doses can negate much, if not all, the benefits. Only after a company has implemented the inexpensive methods already described in this book, which are certain to save much more than they cost, should any major expenditures for new plant or new equipment be considered. In fact, new plant and equipment should be one of the last considerations, if only because a fundamental concept of maximizing profits is to reduce costs, not to make the somewhat contradictory decision to purchase new facilities, thereby adding to debt and depreciation charges, and reducing cash flow. Besides, it is through the profit improvement techniques discussed previously that you will have the available funds to purchase new equipment.

Managers who know how to get peak usage from existing facilities and personnel will be the ones to make the smartest decisions, and get the most benefit, from new equipment and machinery. Before making a large capital expenditure, make certain you are getting maximum usage from the plant and equipment the company already owns. During periods of acquisition and consolidation, many top managers find that they can get three or four times the production from a plant than was the case at the time they inherited it. This increased utilization and productivity can be brought about not only through the use of profit improvement techniques that increase productivity, but by improving methods, adding shifts, selling idle or unnecessary equipment, adjusting layout and work flow, and employing the prudent and efficient techniques of good management.

Experiment with new equipment before committing large sums of money. Make certain you know what you are getting into and act prudently. Don't be too quick to get rid of aging equipment. When the family car breaks down, the first reaction is to fix it, not to buy a new car. The same instincts should be followed in the factory. A robust maintenance program that begins the moment a piece of machinery is purchased is likely to increase its lifespan by many years.

We know of one midsize company that has a policy of never buying brand new equipment. It operates each machine as fast and as hard as possible until it breaks down. The failed part is repaired and strengthened, and the process is repeated until another part fails, is strengthened, and repaired again. This process is repeated until the equipment has essentially been custom redesigned and refurbished, and now operates at three to four times the manufacturer's suggested feeds and speeds or cycle times. This is such a commonsense approach that we often wonder why others don't adopt it.

The Industrial Revolution Redux

The other side of the coin, of course, is that those who fail to participate in the new industrial revolution are going to be left behind, and will have difficulty surviving. While new plants and equipment are by no means a substitute for good management, there are of course many situations in which their purchase is advisable. With the latest in robotics and direct computer controlled machines (DCC), today's modern factory can be totally controlled by a microprocessor, which can not only run the entire manufacturing operation automatically, but also provide an instant evaluation of inventory. This alone reduces both work-in-process inventories and "floor to floor" time. As manufacturing equipment becomes increasingly computerized and automated, in some cases the payback period has become shorter and shorter, thereby increasing the likelihood that new purchases will be cost effective.

The cost of shifting over to the latest technology can be staggering, and obsolescence from ongoing state-of-the-art advancements is rapid. Nevertheless, the potential cost savings are enormous. Not only does the cost of direct and indirect labor and fringes fall, but savings also result from reducing your required square footage, much lower scrap, longer running times, automatic feeds, and a much more rapid processing of inventory.

Payback Calculations

A company had better be certain of the precise benefits -- most specifically, the payback period based on increased productivity -- before spending substantial sums on a new plant or the latest equipment. Many managers assume that they can obtain a quick payback on new equipment. This may very well be the case, but don't be cavalier about this crucial decision.

When trying to decide whether or not to spend large sums of money on new equipment, many companies are satisfied with a payback period of two years. Some companies will accept as many as five. The object is to get the biggest bang for your buck. Set the bar high. There are many situations when expenditures for new equipment can pay for themselves in one year or less. Exhaust every possible analysis before settling for anything longer than that. We consider a two-year payback period to be the maximum you should allow, except in extraordinary circumstances, which do, of course, occur.

Also, be certain that your risk/reward analysis is accurate. All too often the cost analysis to determine the amount of time required until new equipment pays for itself stops after a simple comparison between the old and new equipment's speed and productivity. These are important factors, of course, but there are others to consider as well. For example, the increased efficiency of new equipment will often allow additional volume to be brought in from the outside. Perhaps a previous make-or-buy evaluation concluded that an item could be more profitably purchased from an outside supplier than it could be manufactured internally. Frequently, the added capabilities of a new machine will reduce costs so that the make-or-buy decision can be reevaluated in favor of manufacturing the part in-house. This can reduce overall overhead, and increase sales and profit margins.

Be certain that the new machinery you are purchasing has the flexibility to handle multiple operations. Somewhere down the road you might want to use it to manufacture a similar part, or to make a change in a part you are now manufacturing on an older, less adaptable machine. The precise nature of future requirements may be unknown, but new equipment tends to be designed with flexibility in mind, an element that in the long run can be extremely valuable.

Put simply: try to buy machines that can perform multiple operations. Multi-operation equipment not only reduces the number of total machines that are necessary, but also frees up space and increases inventory turn, since work- in-process (WIP) is reduced. If a particular part is currently manufactured in four or five separate operations by four or five different machines, there is considerable down time, or work-in-process, when a part is sitting idle, waiting to be moved on to the next machine. But the latest generation of machines can frequently manufacture the part in one fluid operation, thereby increasing efficiency and reducing its per unit cost.

Replacing several machines with one new machine will also reduce a plant's square footage requirements. This too might alter a previously-made make-or-buy evaluation, or even enable an entire plant to be closed or consolidated .

Replacing outdated machinery with the latest technology will almost always reduce the total number of machines required in a plant. It is typically a three-to-one relationship; one new machine should be able to replace three old ones. Newer equipment may also eliminate the need for auxiliary machines, such as a hand drill or a small milling device that previously had been kept in a closet until needed. Again, this is a cost savings that is often overlooked when determining the payback period for a particular expenditure.

Be certain also to include in your payback calculations the resale value of the old machinery. Even World War II vintage machinery is usually worth something, even if only for scrap or spare parts.

Exhibit 8-2:
New Plant and Equipment Example

A $100 million manufacturer of high precision stainless steel machine parts purchases a new $2 million machine. The number of persons required for the operation is reduced from 123 to 79, and the number of machine tools is reduced from 80 to 48. What's more, 1.6 million parts, or the equivalent of about 44,000 standard hours, that were being sourced from a third party can now be moved back in-house. The fewer pieces of machinery drop the operation's square footage requirement, and a sister plant is able to be closed and consolidated into this plant. Nineteen months later the new equipment has paid for itself.

Thirty-Day Program

In the previous chapters we have hammered home the idea that since in most manufacturing companies direct labor only represents 5–15 percent of total costs, there are other areas more ripe for maximizing profits. In Chapter 1, for example, we showed how a 5 percent reduction in direct labor costs would increase profits by about a half of one percent, while a 5 percent reduction in material costs will increase profits by more than 2 percent.

This is all true, but it is also true that the cost of direct labor has climbed substantially in recent years, as fringe benefits have begun to take an increasingly larger percentage of the total. Check your factory overhead to see what percentage is made up of fringe costs; it is substantial -- probably in the neighborhood of 40 percent.

Direct labor is also an area that can be addressed quickly, with almost immediate benefits. In fact, we have developed a 30-day program, divided into the first weekend, the first week, and the first month, which should result in immediate and considerable rewards – enough to pay for longer-term, more comprehensive profit improvement efforts. This "quick and dirty" 30-day method utilizes techniques which, if followed, can result in a 5-20 percent reduction in personnel costs (with 10 percent a reasonable target) within a month's time.

As discussed in Chapter 2, the first step of the 30-day program is organizational analysis, which can be initiated during any weekend in the comfort and privacy of one's own home. The only reference material needed is an accurate, up-to-date organization chart that includes the salaries of each employee. Aim for a savings of at least 1-2 percent of sales through reorganization.

Following the first weekend's work on organizational analysis, the next step is to perform a ratio analysis of your total operation, and then of individual departments and expenditures, including direct and indirect labor. As explained in Chapter 1, you can pinpoint specific targeted goals within a week or so after obtaining detailed departmental budget figures from your financial manager.

In most cases, a thirty-day cost reduction program can cut at least 2-5 percent of total sales costs the first time it is conducted. Not only that, similar savings can be accomplished year after year. No single 30-day program will eliminate all the inefficiencies and waste in an organization, and it certainly will not prevent the same problems from turning up again. But regardless of how much waste has been allowed to creep back into your organization in a year's time, you are safe in the knowledge that a continuous, persistent program of organizational analysis and ratio analysis, combined with even an informal work sampling investigation, is costing very little, and thus is a no-risk, but potentially very profitable, strategy which should be repeated at least once a year.

CHAPTER NINE

GROW AND PROSPER

Way back in Chapter 1 we demonstrated that reducing costs is a far easier way to improve profits than increasing sales. That's because growth is expensive, and particularly during periods of high interest rates or tight credit, increasing sales means increasing debt, which can lead to lower profits. In contrast, by implementing certain profit improvement techniques, the results are immediate and dramatic. An increase in sales, in other words, costs a company money, while reducing costs and becoming more efficient do not.

That said, once you have maximized profitability and eliminated the excesses and inefficiencies in your operation, of course you want to grow. But you want to do it while still maintaining your profit margins. There are two ways to do this. You can grow internally, primarily by maximizing your company's profitability and investing the extra cash into expanding product lines and launching more aggressive sales and marketing efforts. Or you can grow externally, primarily by acquiring other companies in a similar or related field.

Nucleus Theory

External growth also may mean expanding from your initial line of business and creating a larger, more diversified company. One way to do that is the way Harry E. Figgie Jr. built a $1 billion company virtually from scratch   through what he called the nucleus theory of growth. His nucleus theory is based on the idea of acquiring companies in industries experiencing better than average growth, then building within those industries by acquiring related companies. The first acquisition within each growth industry is called the nucleus.

Additional companies in that industry are then added in order to complement and expand the nucleus.

The nucleus theory is essentially the selection, acquisition, and internal development of companies within major industries and with complementary product lines. Growth prospects for each nucleus industry must in some way be quantifiable, either by determining that its products will fill a continuing need in the economy, or that new products of particular benefit can be identified, developed, and marketed. Each nucleus should represent an industry dominated by a number of small and medium-size firms rather than one or two giants.

The original nucleus company should also be in a growth field in which foreign competition will not be a factor for the foreseeable future, and in which you have some expertise. Before more companies are added, each nucleus company that is acquired should be doing at least $40 million in sales. Anything below that, you sneeze and you're out of business. Small companies have all the problems of large companies, but less money, time, and manpower to find the solutions. Harry used to like to quote Cash McCall,[22] who said: "Successful companies come in two sizes these days. Small and large. It's the medium-sized ones that have the tough go -- too big to be handled with one-man management, not big enough to support a real organization."

From a $40 million start, the goal should be to build each nucleus as quickly as possible, mostly through acquisitions, until they reach $200 million in sales. Ideally the companies you acquire should have sales of $40 million, but sometimes this is easier said than done. At the beginning of your acquisitions program, you may only be able to afford smaller, ailing businesses. You'll have to be confident that by using the profit improvement strategies spelled out in the previous pages, you will be able to nurse them to $40 million before growing the nucleus to $200 million and more. Try to focus on industries in

---

22. Cash McCall is the fictional title character of "Cash McCall" by Cameron Hawley, first published by Houghton Mifflin in 1955.

which a $150-$200 million nucleus will constitute a position of considerable importance.

The nucleus theory provides flexibility in deciding what kinds of businesses to enter. It offers a central, coordinated theme that can consistently be explained to the media, security analysts, and most importantly, the owners and employees of potential acquisitions. It will also allow you to organize the company along product lines, and develop expertise and market share in a handful of growth industries. That knowledge can then be used to increase market share.

The nucleus theory also provides an excellent framework for management in that related divisions can be managed at the corporate level by a group executive familiar both with the overall market and specific product lines. It allows for a small, highly mobile corporate staff to place responsibility for profit-making decisions at the division level. Each division president has entrepreneurial-like control of his company's fortunes, including profit and growth targets. In this streamlined organization, a division president reports to a group vice president, who in turn reports directly to the CEO.

As the overall company matures, its combination of size and diversification should protect it from the fluctuations of any one industry or division, and provide a balance in every kind of financial climate. In a diversified company with four, five, or six nuclei, it's difficult to come up with a scenario in which each business would experience a downturn simultaneously. Today, with so much competition and short product life cycles, the benefits of diversification have never been greater. It's better to walk on six legs than on one or two.

Choosing Acquisitions

When looking for potential acquisitions, pay particular attention to their growth potential. Look for companies that fit into a nucleus you have already established, or one which you are interested in starting. Always be on the lookout for concerns which are not so blue chip that you cannot afford them, but not so sick that they will not be susceptible to your profit improvement program.

Once you identify a company worthy of consideration, schedule a face-to-face meeting with its owner and other top management. Have your chief engineer inspect the plant floor and every piece of machinery and method. Have the head of your accounting department ask for the company's profit and loss statements for the past half dozen years, and have your top human resources person evaluate the labor situation. Looking at the big picture, value companies the same way you would a new piece of equipment (see Chapter 8), by how long it should take to pay back the purchase price from earnings. Many people today are using EBITDA (earnings before interest, taxes, depreciation, and amortization), but that's a financial guy's measurement. Instead, we always look for payback and cash flow, which we consider an entrepreneur's measurement. Cash flow is your lifeline, so learn how to calculate and quantify it.

In making your calculations, past performance should never be as important as perceived potential. For that you have to rely on what you can learn about the efficiency of the company's manufacturing process, labor situation, and what your own experience tells you can be done to improve the company's bottom line. Sometimes your reasons for rejecting a company may be unorthodox, but they should always be based on past experience, translated into simple common sense. One time we passed on a deal after our chief engineer warned us that the company we had visited had morale problems. There was heavy drinking going on. How did he know? He noticed empty liquor bottles wedged in between the wire mesh protecting the plant's windows.

Try also to determine the company's reputation, which you can usually do over the internet or with a few phone calls. Ask yourself whether it has a powerful brand, and if its financials are in line with the rest of the industry. And finally, try to find out why a company is for sale. Is it because the entire industry is in trouble? Is a competitor taking it to the cleaners? Or is it a more positive reason, like perhaps the owners want to take their money out after a lifetime of building the company, or they feel the need to become part of a larger company in order to compete in the marketplace. Ultimately, the choice of which companies to investigate, and then which to buy, will likely rest more on your instincts than on any quantifiable evaluation.

Assume that most companies for sale are overpriced. But if the price is comparable to what other companies in that same industry have sold for, then the only important determination is whether or not you will be able to recoup the cost of the purchase from profits in a reasonable period of time.

Our payback calculations may be slightly different than most, particularly when purchasing a company in order to add a product line or expertise -- what we call "tuck-in" acquisitions. In this case we suggest calculating payback for an acquisition based on the earnings of the new combined company, since the reason you made the acquisition in the first place was to help the entire nucleus. If you are following the nucleus theory of growth, tuck-in acquisitions are often designed to increase the competitive position of an existing division, or to increase its size so that it reaches one of your minimum divisional sales targets. Some consolidations might reduce short-term profits, but all of them should take advantage of economies of scale.

When there is a wide difference of opinion about how much a company is worth, either walk away from the deal, or offer an earn-out over a period of years based on future performance. In that way if the company performs as well as the owners predict, they will eventually get their price, while if it doesn't perform up to expectations, you are protected.

Personal Approach to Negotiation

Sometimes one's style of negotiation is more important than even price, particularly if the owners you are negotiating with are the entrepreneurial founders. In this case, they may want to sell their company, but they may also want to maintain their position as president, at least until they retire. They will also likely feel a responsibility to their employees, some of whom may have worked for them for many years and whom they consider family. In this case, the owners will want to make a deal that will have the company continue to operate independently even after they are out of the picture. Under these circumstances, be aware that giving up ownership was probably the most significant thing the seller will ever do in their business lives. Go out of your way to assure them that the sale of their company is not only good for them and their families financially, but will ultimately be good for the company and its employees. Then be sure to follow through on these promises.

Particularly when negotiating with entrepreneurial founders, it will often be to your advantage to sit across the negotiating table from them in order to personally make them understand that this is an important transaction for you too, and that you are counting on them to be an important part of something bigger than their company alone. This commitment will give you an advantage over other suitors. Your interest in retaining current management and allowing them to operate their company independently will be appealing to many owners. It is also good business. Regard management as an important asset, and express and demonstrate your eagerness to make certain they remain with you. The personnel at the companies you acquire will be the most important asset you are buying. Be careful not to alienate them. A mass exodus of employees at a newly acquired company could prove disastrous for an already thinly stretched corporate staff.

Striking a Balance

You have to continually strike a balance between jumping right into a new acquisition to make certain its management takes the steps necessary to improve profitability, and allowing them to utilize their expertise to the fullest. In most cases, one of the most important criteria in choosing an acquisition will be the quality of the people in charge. After the sale you will want to give them the decision-making authority to run their own companies. They will know their company better than you; your job will be to add your own expertise to the mix. In fact, unless you are using it as a tuck-in acquisition, and interested only in a particular product line, we would not even recommend buying a company if management does not agree to stay. They know their company better than anyone you could bring in.

Retaining current management, advising them in the profit improvement strategies detailed in this text, but giving them the autonomy to operate their own entrepreneurial enterprise without heavy corporate overhead, can become a key ingredient in your growth strategy. You might also want to offer a compensation plan that includes generous incentive bonuses for excellent performance. In effect, you are offering people the opportunity to build a larger, more successful business.

Exerting control at the corporate level and giving division presidents as much autonomy as they can handle can be a difficult balance to maintain, but it will be crucial to your external growth plans. Allow each division to operate independently, at least until it proves it cannot do so profitably or is not properly implementing your profit improvement strategies. Stay sensitive to former corporate management's desire to remain autonomous. At the same time, impress upon them the need to make important changes aimed at maximizing profitability. But while your fresh perspective will be invaluable, remember too that your own corporate staff could not possibly understand a division's business as well as the people who have been working there for years, sometimes for all their professional lives. For at least the first year, jump into only the most severe problem areas at divisions performing poorly.

Hardcore

Once your acquisition program is underway and you find yourself operating multiple companies, particularly if they are in different businesses, you will need a way to keep careful tabs on their performance, while at the same time allowing them their independence. One way to do that is through a system of annual "hardcore" meetings. Every Fall, the company president and financial manager should meet with the management team of the parent company to outline their plans for the upcoming year, and for the four years after that. Consider these hardcore sessions sacrosanct, a contract between the division president and corporate. Expect division presidents to prepare for them by understanding every detail of their business. Be tough. Test their acumen by choosing one particular subject in their vast array of data, and expect a good answer to why something had or had not occurred, not only in the year projected, but the current year, and perhaps in the last five years on display, or even five years into the future. Expect the people running every profit center to know their operations inside and out.

Use the hardcore meetings to make certain all company or division presidents understand and are implementing every profit improvement strategy described in this book. Once that is underway, they might find they are able to meet a more ambitious financial performance than they first proposed. At the same time, be certain they are being realistic about their projections. You want them to be confident that they can meet their sales and profit projections. By helping them deliver what they promised, you can meet your own cash planning and other financial estimates.

Try to establish a competitive environment that rewards financial achievement. Be aware, however, that there is something psychologically tempting about trying to impress corporate with ambitious projections. One way to temper that enthusiasm is to tie incentive bonuses directly to how much the division exceeds its hardcore projections. That way there is no reason to over task, since the compensation of employees is directly related to how well the hardcore projections are fulfilled.

You might find that some divisions will have to revise their hardcore plan several times before it is accepted. Try to turn the hardcore sessions into mini profit improvement seminars. Before long, hardcore will be looked forward to by those presidents performing well, but dreaded by those who consistently fall short of their projections. If a company head misses a projection two or three years in a row, take a hard look at that person's ability to continue managing the company.

CHAPTER TEN

FOR THE REST OF YOUR LIFE

Perhaps a final chapter should be added to this guide entitled "Maintaining Profit Improvement as a Continuing Priority." The chapter could consist of one sentence only: "Now turn to page 1 and begin your program again."

The temptation, after improving profits by 20, 30, 40 percent or more, is to feel that your company is now operating at peak efficiency and maximum profitability. This is dangerous, and is as unrealistic as it is costly. Without ongoing surveillance, excess personnel, wasteful habits, and countless other inefficiencies will begin to creep back into your operation within a very short period of time. For this reason, and because no profit improvement program can eliminate all the unnecessary fat the first time around, you will be surprised to find that significant improvements in your operations can be made year after year, no matter how long your profit improvement program has been underway. Even in a well-run operation, an ongoing comprehensive program should save you an additional 4-5 percent of costs annually, each and every year.

Day after day, week after week, year after year, your company must be continually prepared to thwart the many routine business practices that tend to encourage waste. Your company must, for example, make certain, almost on a daily basis, that its pricing structure is not giving away all (or more) of the savings that have been gained through your profit improvement efforts (Chapter 7), that appropriate emphasis is being placed on the purchasing department (Chapters 3 and 4), and that costly capital expenditures (Chapter 8) are not being made before more cost effective internal measures are implemented.

Many company presidents may feel ill equipped to implement every one of these techniques by themselves. Presidents who have come up the ranks through sales may not feel competent to lead the charge on a make-or-buy decision. Or perhaps a chief executive with a financial background does not feel sufficiently familiar with the engineering department to determine whether a design change is warranted. But as the top executive, you do not need to be an expert in every profit improvement strategy. You <u>do</u> need to understand their basic rationale and goals so you can ask the right questions and act on the answers. Challenge your department heads to submit specific profit improvement recommendations. If, for example, your engineering manager tells you that his department is operating at 100 percent efficiency and that it would be impossible to streamline the operation, you may have to resort to suggesting that an across-the-board reduction in overhead will have to be implemented. This should prompt the department manager to take another look at the situation.

Coordinate your company's comprehensive profit improvement effort with your entire organization by holding meetings attended by all department heads. It is your job to take a look at the total picture. If you pass this responsibility to your subordinates, you are going to lose the synergism of picking up savings between departments. With everyone sitting around the table, ask them, "Are there any combined improvements that can be implemented?" One department may have a person who is only effective half the time but is nevertheless vital to the operation. A similar situation may exist in another department, in which case two half-time jobs, currently being performed by two persons, could be altered so that they both are filled by one employee. Two or more executives might be able to share a secretary, for example. Or perhaps one part of the production team is unaware that there is excess capacity on a particular machine. Effective communications is key here.

Once a comprehensive profit improvement effort is underway, the drive to make these techniques a top priority -- a way of life – is crucial.

Their importance must be truly understood not only by yourself, but by every person being paid by the company. All employees should be assigned to a cost improvement team which is given a monetary goal to be realized in the current calendar year. Each team should include at least one major department manager and, to the extent practical, team members should be related by department assignment or job content. Team captains can report to a cost improvement administrator, appointed by the company president. The administrator's responsibilities include:

1. Ensuring an adequate supply of cost reduction dockets (like the one depicted in Exhibit 10-1).
2. Routing copies of the completed dockets to all department managers impacted by the suggestions.
3. Insuring timely evaluation of every profit improvement suggestion.
4. Preparing and distributing a monthly summary of the suggestions.
5. Preparing and distributing a quarterly list of all salaried employees, ranked in order of the monetary value of their suggestions that are implemented.

The key here is to get *everyone* involved in the effort to cut costs and improve profits. The many people responsible for the hundreds of details in an industrial operation are in the best position to take the steps necessary to make their own areas more efficient. These men and women know better than anyone else about their particular job functions. Make a concerted effort to extract that knowledge and to implement it in a way that improves profits. In fact, assign all salaried workers to a cost reduction team. As a condition of employment, require them to submit cost reduction suggestions in writing, using a form similar to the one presented as Exhibit 10-1. Insist on 100 percent participation, and tie salary increases directly to an employee's cost reduction contributions.

Although some jobs, such as engineering and purchasing, are more conducive to profit improvement than others, no job is immune. You will find that the profit improvement ideas among your employees will range widely in both scope and substance. Exhibits 10-2, 10-3, and 10-4 offer three real examples of the virtually limitless kinds of suggestions you can expect.

It is the *attitude* that is important, not the amount of money involved. While the overall objective is to reduce costs and maximize profits by as much as possible, the real goal is to encourage all employees to persistently and continually think of ways in which costs can be reduced, and therefore profits maximized, in their particular area of employment.

Publicly recognize each accepted cost improvement suggestion with a certificate of achievement. Additional recognition can be given to employees who reach milestones of five, ten, fifteen, and twenty accepted suggestions. And make an accepted cost or profit improvement suggestion one condition of any merit salary increase.

Exhibit 10-1: Cost Improvement Docket

TOTAL ESTIMATED SAVINGS (ANNUALIZED)		DOCKET NO.	
COST OF IMPLEMENTING DOCKET		DEPARTMENT NO.	
ANNUAL NET SAVINGS		DATE	
TYPE OF DOCKET:		SUBMITTED BY:	
		APPROVED BY:	
PRODUCT ☐	MANAGED ☐	APPROVED BY:	

DESCRIPTION

ASSIGNMENT OF RESPONSIBILITY			
DATE	ASSIGNED TO	SCHEDULE OF ACTIVITY	RESULTS

THIS DOCKET IS: DATE _____

☐ APPROVED FOR _____

☐ DROPPED BECAUSE _____

Exhibit 10-2: Cost Improvement Docket Example 1

TOTAL ESTIMATED SAVINGS (ANNUALIZED)	$1,200	DOCKET NO.	
COST OF IMPLEMENTING DOCKET	0	DEPARTMENT NO.	Sales
ANNUAL NET SAVINGS	$1,200	DATE	
TYPE OF DOCKET:		SUBMITTED BY:	
		APPROVED BY:	
PRODUCT ☐ MANAGED ☒		APPROVED BY:	

DESCRIPTION
When making airplane reservations for Mr. W. to travel
to Los Angeles, I obtained a 33 percent senior citizen
discount. The total cost of the ticket without the
discount was $718.00; the cost with the 33 percent discount
was $478.00, a total savings of $240.00. The estimated
annual savings will be five times this amount.

ASSIGNMENT OF RESPONSIBILITY			
DATE	ASSIGNED TO	SCHEDULE OF ACTIVITY	RESULTS

Exhibit 10-3: Cost Improvement Docket Example 2

TOTAL ESTIMATED SAVINGS (ANNUALIZED)	$11,266	DOCKET NO.	
COST OF IMPLEMENTING DOCKET		DEPARTMENT NO.	
ANNUAL NET SAVINGS		DATE	
TYPE OF DOCKET:		SUBMITTED BY:	
		APPROVED BY:	
PRODUCT ☑ MANAGED ☐		APPROVED BY:	

DESCRIPTION
By unitizing test leads for
a product into a single fixture,
20 minutes per unit is saved during
adjustment and final testing.
Originally, test leads were connected
individually in such a way that often
produced a short.
Total Units = 5,633 units
20 minutes/unit = 1877.67 hours x $6/hour = $11,266

ASSIGNMENT OF RESPONSIBILITY			
DATE	ASSIGNED TO	SCHEDULE OF ACTIVITY	RESULTS

THIS DOCKET IS: DATE _____

☐ APPROVED FOR _____

☐ DROPPED BECAUSE _____

Exhibit 10-4: Cost Improvement Docket Example 3

TOTAL ESTIMATED SAVINGS (ANNUALIZED)	$19,069.88	DOCKET NO.	
COST OF IMPLEMENTING DOCKET		DEPARTMENT NO.	Engineering
ANNUAL NET SAVINGS	$19,069.88	DATE	
TYPE OF DOCKET:		SUBMITTED BY:	
		APPROVED BY:	
PRODUCT ☒ MANAGED ☐		APPROVED BY:	

DESCRIPTION		
Change terminals in B3 series bases to one piece,		
removing two part numbers from stock. Terminals cannot be		
torqued out of base.		
Part numbers removed	$1.29 per base part savings	$818.40
35180-1 3 per 1.16 each	Removing two part numbers	$50.00
35400-1 3 per .36 each. 1.52 each x 3 4.56 per base	Scrap rate 40%	15,265.80
	Base labor saving 20 min	163.68
	Line labor savings 2 hrs	2772.00
35177-1 6 per .22 each		$19,069.88
35401-1 6 per .24 each 1.01 x 6 $6.06		

ASSIGNMENT OF RESPONSIBILITY			
DATE	ASSIGNED TO	SCHEDULE OF ACTIVITY	RESULTS

THIS DOCKET IS: DATE _____

☐ APPROVED FOR _____

☐ DROPPED BECAUSE _____

Exhibit 10-5 Cost Reduction Teams

1.
 1. Superintendant, Machine Shop
 2. Foreman
 3. Foreman

2.
 1. Supervisor, Assembly Depts.
 2. Foreman
 3. Foreman
 4. Foreman
 5. Foreman
 6. Foreman
 7. Foreman
 8. Foreman
 9. Jr. Engineer

3.
 1. Supervisor, Process Engineer
 2. Process Engineer
 3. Maintenance Foreman

4.
 1. Purchasing Manager
 2. Senior Buyer
 3. Administrative Assistant
 4. Foreman, Quality Assurance

5.
 1. Manufacturing Manager
 2. Supervisor, Storeroom
 3. Production Planner
 4. Production Scheduler
 5. Computer Operator
 6. Keypunch Operator
 7. Production Scheduler
 8. Supervisor, Data Processing

6.
 1. Engineering Manager
 2. Engineering Data Coordinator
 3. Supervisor, Drafting
 4. Draftsman
 5. Project Engineer
 6. Project Engineer
 7. Project Engineer
 8. Project Engineer
 9. Project Engineer
 10. Engineering Section Manager
 11. Design Engineer
 12. Engineer 1
 13. Engineer 2
 14. Engineer 3
 15. Engineer 4
 16. Engineer 5
 17. Engineer 6
 18. Administrative Assistant

7.
 1. V.P. Marketing
 2. Contracts Manager
 3. Supervisor, Order Service
 4. Sales Engineer
 5. Customer Service Agent
 6. Executive Secretary
 7. Secretary
 8. Sales Engineer

8.
 1. Controller (financial manager)
 2. Secretary
 3. Secretary
 4. Jr. Accountant

ABOUT THE AUTHORS

Harry E. Figgie Jr., grew up in Cleveland in the 1930s. He lost his father in 1940 at the age of sixteen and five years later was fighting in General Patton's Third Army with an infantry division in Europe. After returning home, he finished his last two years of undergraduate work with a Bachelor's in metallurgical engineering. He then received an MBA from Harvard as a member of the Class of 1949, which Larry Shames, in his 1974 book about the class, called "the most wildly successful batch of MBAs to have shared a campus anywhere, ever."[23] Along the way he also earned a law degree and a masters in industrial engineering by going to night school while working full time in various sales and manufacturing positions.

---

23. "The Big Time: Harvard Business School's Most Successful Class--And How It Shaped America" by Laurence Shames, Harpercollins, 1986.

From 1953 until 1962 Mr. Figgie worked at the consulting firm, Booz Allen Hamilton, where he became one of the country's leading cost reduction experts. He then used this expertise to build Figgie International from a struggling $23 million sprinkler company into a consistently profitable, $1.3 billion diversified corporation. He used tried and true methods that are just as effective today as they were then -- common sense measures like ratio analysis and work sampling, ABC inventory control, product redesign, and a focus on those areas where the company was spending most of its money. Most importantly, he implemented fundamental changes to eliminate waste and improve efficiencies that became part of each company's normal mode of operations.

Mr. Figgie is the author of the bestseller, *Bankruptcy 1995* in which he warned America of the dangers of high deficits and profligate government spending. It sold more than 300,000 copies and was on the *New York Times* bestseller list for almost a year. He is also the author of *Building a Billion Dollar Company From Scratch* (Ruder Finn Press, 2008) and the successful *Cutting Costs: An Executive's Guide to Increased Profits* (AMACOM, 1990), much of which has been revised and incorporated into *Maximizing Profits Immediately*.

Mr. Figgie's management strategies continue to be utilized and updated by his son, Matthew, and those who work for the Clark-Reliance Corporation, the company the Figgie family has owned for more than 50 years. For more information about Mr. Figgie's background and expertise, visit harryefiggiejr.com.

Matthew P. Figgie is Chairman of the Clark-Reliance Corporation. For many years before that he was the company's Vice President of Mergers, Acquisitions and Corporate Investments. He also served as Interim President of Clark-Reliance before the appointment of Rick Solon. He is the President and CEO of Figgie Capital, a diversified investment company.

Mr. Figgie is a member of the board of directors at a number of other companies, including American Fire Group, BGI Broadcasting, Icon Management Systems, and Marri Broadcasting. He previously held the position of Director of Mergers and Acquisitions and Corporate Investments at the public company, Figgie International. And he is currently Chairman of the Figgie Foundation.

An Ohio resident, Matthew Figgie received his B.S. from The McIntire School of Business at The University of Virginia and his B.A. from Baldwin Wallace College. He has an MBA from The Weatherhead School of Management at Case Western Reserve University.

As Chairman of Clark-Reliance, Mr. Figgie is continuing his father's strategy of internal growth through product expansion and the profit improvement strategies described in *Maximizing Profits Immediately*, and through strategic external growth centered on the senior Figgie's nucleus theory.

Richard A. Solon has more than 30 years of experience in manufacturing and operations. Hired and trained by Harry E. Figgie Jr. in 1975, Mr. Solon was enrolled in the first management training program at Figgie International, where for four years he rotated among various divisions, being exposed to almost every business discipline. That is also when he first began to study modern management theories and techniques and recognized how in many cases they seemed to be spun off of the principles and techniques espoused in Mr. Figgie's *Cutting Costs* guide, first published in 1983.

In the various stops during his business career Mr. Solon has repeatedly used the profit improvement methods discussed in *Maximizing Profits Immediately* to build a track record of sales and profit growth successes. After spending the first 24 years of his career at Figgie

International, Mr. Solon was for three years President and CEO of Orion Bus (a DaimlerChrysler company) before rejoining the Figgie family as President and CEO of the Clark-Reliance Corporation.

Adam C. Snyder, a freelance business writer, worked with Harry E. Figgie Jr. on a number of writing projects, including *Building a Billion Dollar Company From Scratch* and *Cutting Costs: An Executive's Guide to Increased Profits*. Mr. Snyder has also collaborated, co-authored, or ghost written many other business and inspirational books with top CEOs and business leaders. He is also president of the animation company, Rembrandt Films LLC. For more information about him and his company, visit www.rembrandtfilms.com.

INDEX

www.ingramcontent.com/pod-product-compliance
Lightning Source LLC
Chambersburg PA
CBHW080248200526
45166CB00021B/319